Portraits of the Artist

The Self-Portrait in Painting

Portraits of the Artist

The Self-Portrait in Painting

by

Pascal Bonafoux

SKIRA

RIZZOLI
NEW YORK

© 1985 by Editions d'Art Albert Skira S.A., Geneva

Published in the United States of America in 1985 by

RIZZOLI INTERNATIONAL PUBLICATIONS, INC.
712 Fifth Avenue/New York 10019

Reproduction rights reserved by A.D.A.G.P. and
S.P.A.D.E.M., Paris, and Cosmopress, Geneva

Printed in Switzerland

Library of Congress Cataloging in Publication Data
Bonafoux, Pascal.
    Portraits of the artist.

    Translation of: Les peintres et l'autoportrait.
    Bibliography: p.
    Includes index.
    1. Self-portraits.   2. Portrait paintings–Themes,
motives.   I. Title.
ND1300.B613   1985   757'.3   84-43073
ISBN 0-8478-0586-7

Et direxi me ad me et dixi mihi:
Tu qui es?
Et respondi ...

St. Augustine
Confessions

When they did their portrait,
they did it looking at each other in a mirror,
without realizing that they themselves were a
mirror.

Paul Eluard
Donner à voir, 1939

Filippino Lippi: *Self-Portrait, c. 1485*

Lightning conductor

*A preface might be called a lightning
conductor.*

Lichtenberg
Aphorisms, I, 1775-1779

... per visibilia ad invisibilia.
St. Paul

It was a self-portrait sketch of Filippino Lippi
that started it all off. There are questions to be answered. (There is no certainty that they concern this
portrait alone. *I myself* have a role to play.) And
these questions, like the self-portrait sketch itself,
are incomplete and uncertain. Here doubt is pertinent – doubt alone is appropriate – and imper-
tinent – as an expression of arrogance. The portrait
is a refusal: it refuses to own up to any assurance,
any assertion that it is more than an anecdote. The
portrait is also a challenge: this portrait provokes
questions and rejects the answers or only tolerates
them as hypotheses. This refusal and this challenge
are an expression of duality; the portrait, the sitter,
and the mirror that isn't there which they imply,
"are perfect likenesses of each other, although no
one can say which one conferred its likeness on the
other."[1] The mirror – a necessary intermediary –
has been eluded, conjured away, the portrait completed. Rather than eluded, we ought to say elided;
the mirror has been replaced by an apostrophe. The
portrait accosts us: Who am I? Know thyself! Is the

portrait of the painter by himself the response given
to this question and this command?

Near the suspended frame enclosing the portrait,
or set in the moulding of the frame itself, is a copper
plate engraved in roman capitals; the same title
repeated: Portrait of the painter by himself. (We
should investigate the implication and underlying
substance or significance of these words "title" and
"legend." The *title* of the picture becomes the *legend*
of its photographic reproduction. Titles are intended for works of art, legends for photographs...
Title: the word designates an honour, a degree and
a name. Legend: the word designates a fable and a
comment. The portrait of the painter by himself,
both title and legend, convey the meanings concealed by these words: honour *or* fable, honour *and*
fable... and no contradiction exists...) The dates
change: Portrait of the painter by himself 1450,
1498, 1527, 1538, 1564, 1587, 1606, 1634, 1638...
1787, 1793... 1824... 188... 1918... 1954...
1971. The names change. Lippi, Raphael, Ban-
dinelli, Rubens, Rembrandt, Gauguin, Mondrian,
Man Ray. The painter will have changed his
pseudonym... A word is engraved on the plate
which refers to a mirror suspended on the wall:

7

SELF-PORTRAIT. In the *Dictionnaire de l'Académie des Beaux-Arts* (Paris, 1864), "containing words which belong to the teaching, practice and history of the Fine Arts," the word "autoportrait" (self-portrait) does not appear . . . Portrait of the painter by himself, self-portrait, a constant in art. The painter has never ceased to portray himself. In the thirteenth century he appears in the margins of manuscripts; in the twentieth century it is, *inter alia*, a mirror that he proffers as a self-portrait.

> How joyous would my spirits be
> If this were still the age
> Of metamorphosis;
> Granting I too were changed
> Into a bright illumined glass
> Such as frozen snows bring forth!
> Oh mirror! I crave and crave
> To dwell like thee in bliss.[2]

Taking the story of the evolution of the self-portrait from the margins of manuscripts to the mirror itself, can we then affirm that this is the story of this metamorphosis which was constantly attempted and ever-recurrent from one century to the next? Was it a unique ambition, ceaselessly rejected which finally became possible after seven centuries of demand and tension? What is self-portrayal? Is the self-portrait the portrait of a mirror? Which mirror is it that poses for the portrait?

> *Its speech is indeed silent,*
> *but every part of it breathes words.*
> Félibien

The painter's name and age are inscribed on the canvas. A certain name made it: "*fecit*" or "*faciebat.*" "*Ætatis suae,*" followed by a figure. "*Fecit; suae.*" Made this picture; his age; in the third person singular. This portrait is the portrait of someone else. The painter paints a painter. I paints himmyself, the sitter. The portrait remains one of another person; it is one portrait among many.

For a long time the self-portrait was a constant feature of the portrait gallery; the painter was the model – and it is the well-known model who makes the decision as to the genre – and this difference alone was enough to determine what this portrait would be, but which could not alter the genre. The fact that this portrait was repeated unendingly changed nothing; what remained was a mere hackneyed stereotype, a sign of complacency.

We may ask if the self-portrait is nothing other than the recurrent portrait of Narcissus, a monotonous repetition.

Maria Ormani: *Illuminated page of a Breviarium cum calendario, Florence, 1453, with self-portrait in lower margin*

> *It is my firm conviction that everyone*
> *differs in his vision of all the visual*
> *elements embodied in a work of art.*
> Roger de Piles

Did Apelles never portray himself? Did Parrhasios paint himself as Hermes? Did Phidias bequeath his own likeness to us? Plutarch answers yes; and he adds Theodoros to the list. Pausanias, similarly, states that Cheirisophos of Crete left a self-portrait. The portraits have vanished, only the texts are extant.[3] And although both Pliny and Boccaccio declare that one of the renowned women, a painter named Marcia, painted a self-portrait, the only extant trace of Marcia painting her own portrait is in an illuminated manuscript on "Noble and Famous Women" copied and illustrated in 1401-1402 for the Duke of Berry.[4] All that antiquity has handed down is this apocryphal self-portrait (and the much worn, and quite forgotten, bas-relief of Archedemos of Thera).

But Tiepolo was to paint himself as Apelles, Rembrandt as Zeuxis, and in 1827 Ingres was to produce a likeness of Apelles as Raphael's guide. Their absence was to remain an obsession, a reference invoked from one century to the next; a model and a warning.

Maria Ormani depicted herself in an attitude of prayer. Calling herself "a maidservant of Christ," she signed and dated the eighty-ninth leaf of a *Breviarium cum calendario*.[5] In the margin of the written text, she states: *scripsit*, "she wrote it."

Boccaccio's Book of Noble and Famous Women:
Marcia painting her own Portrait, 1401-1402

Masaccio and Filippino Lippi:
*St. Peter on his Chair, surrounded by
Brethren, invokes the Holy Ghost,
1426-1427 and 1484*

Filippino Lippi:
*St. Peter raising
the Son of the King
of Antioch from the Dead, 1484*

Filippino Lippi:
*St. Peter and St. Paul
before the Proconsul
and Crucifixion of St. Peter, 1484*

1. Masaccio: *Self-Portrait (from St. Peter on his Chair)*,
   1426-1427
2. Filippino Lippi: *Self-Portrait (from St. Peter and
   St. Paul before the Proconsul)*, *1484*
3. Filippo Lippi: *Self-Portrait (from The Coronation
   of the Virgin)*, *1441-1447*

Filippo Lippi: *The Coronation of the Virgin, 1441-1447*

Standing to the right of *St. Peter on his Chair*, in the Brancacci Chapel of Santa Maria del Carmine in Florence, painted in 1426-1427, Masaccio portrays himself in three-quarter profile, glancing at you as you look at the fresco. And on the opposite wall, with his face similarly angled, adjacent to the Emperor on his throne, thus echoing Masaccio's position adjacent to St. Peter on the throne of the Church, we find Filippino Lippi bordering the frescos he executed to complete the chapel after Masaccio's death. No text, no signature; the only difference lies in the glance aimed at the viewer of the fresco. The painter has advanced from the margins of manuscripts to the borders of the fresco or the altarpiece. A tonsured monk propping up his head, Filippino Lippi's father Fra Filippo Lippi is present at the Coronation of the Virgin but, with a faraway gaze, looks away from it. Contemporary with the appearance of this portrait, unnamed and designated only by the outward glance towards the spectator, another pattern emerges: the painter is alone and named. This is the case with Fouquet. Ten years at most separate Lippi in the midst of a crowd from Fouquet by himself.

Jean Fouquet:
Self-Portrait, c. 1450

11

Giorgione: *Self-Portrait, c. 1500-1510*

Wenzel Hollar: *Giorgione as David holding the Severed Head of Goliath, 1650*

Lippi, like Fouquet, is only a painter because of the works he left us: there is nothing to define this monk or this man wearing a cap as a painter. Nothing in writing, no attributes. The appearance of the painter's attributes is a late phenomenon: brushes, palette, portfolio... The anonymity refused at the outset, refuted by the expression, does not yet amount to identity itself. Now the only portraits are those of donors or princes, but the attributes of painting are lacking. The picture frames behind Poussin and the closed portfolio are severe understatement; and in the apartments of the king's first painter, palette, sketches, small models, sculptures, finished canvases, as well as a collection of various objects, demonstrate that the painter is the equal of anyone. This display, this ostentation are in keeping with the splendours of the court ceremonial in France. In the same century the painter in Holland showed himself at work or surrounded by his family. The Dutch painter belonged to a guild which was just one among many. You could be a painter or a tradesman, there was no difference. In the showiness of pomposity, or in the light of reported evidence, it was always the painter as a member of the social order who was the subject of the portrait.

A little earlier Giorgione represented himself as David holding the severed head of Goliath; and Caravaggio is the severed head of Goliath held out by David.

Neither Giorgione/David nor Caravaggio/Goliath were members of a social order. What then is the painter?

The portrait of the painter by himself is this cleavage, this rift between identity and belonging. Painting oneself is equivalent to painting alluvial deposits and rifts – equivalent to painting belonging and difference. What is the history of the self-portrait? Is it continuous? Is it discontinuous?

*Authentic history being concerned
with everything, the true historian
is concerned with everything.*

Victor Hugo

One person wears a certain type of cap or bonnet; and the type of cap, the headgear worn, is not neutral. Another wears a dark ribbon round his

Caravaggio: *David holding the Head of Goliath, c. 1605-1606*

Francisco Goya: *Self-Portrait*
(from The Count of Floridablanca and Goya, 1783)

Francisco Goya:
Self-Portrait at the Age of Sixty-nine, 1815

wrist; and the "gallant" is not neutral. Another pictures himself as a painter working on somebody's portrait; and the portrait on the easel is not neutral. Yet another person parts his hair in the middle or leaves a strand of his hair longer than the rest, cut to shoulder length; and whether there is a parting or a strand, the hair-style is not neutral. One man comments on his portrait by means of a painted text, a comment on the portrait itself; and the text is not neutral. The next man paints himself in some specific attitude; and the painted gesture is not neutral. There are those who surround themselves with miscellaneous objects scattered about the painted space; and not one of the painted objects is neutral. The costume, the written words, the attitude, none of these is a matter of chance; not one of the details is secondary. It is all a cipher, bearing the seal of identity; everything that is *impressed* upon the portrait must be deciphered. Analysis dissects; and at the same time, analysis records those elements which it can only flutter against or brush past. To analyse is also to test out assumptions and to confute hasty conclusions. There is no certainty

that the presence of Velázquez in *Las Meninas* had the same significance for Goya as it has *for us*. Dürer painted a self-portrait. Cézanne painted a self-portrait. Cézanne painting Cézanne is painting more *a* Cézanne than a portrait *of* Cézanne, whereas the portrait of Dürer is first and foremost a portrait *of* Dürer before it is *a* Dürer *by* Dürer. Which of them is the more present for us? Their portraits do not convey the same presence. Both, through their portraits, are speaking in terms of painting, but Dürer, who corrected the inscription with which he signed the finished work, by writing "*faciebat*" instead of "*fecit*," when he learned that Apelles, according to Pliny, dated his works in this manner using the imperfect tense, was, by doing what he did, stating an implicit genealogy. The matter here is Painting, and Apelles is a challenge. From Apelles to Dürer the line is unbroken; from Dürer to Apelles the proclaimed similarity is a matter of emulation. And Cézanne invents Cézanne; his painting is no longer Painting. Which of the two, Dürer or Cézanne, speaks more of painting? The portrait of the painter by himself is dual: it is *of* and *by*; it concerns the identity of the painter *and* is about painting. Which comes first?

Goya greeting Count Floridablanca to whom he is presenting his portrait is *in our eyes* only an anecdote: in 1783 this court painter is of no interest to us. Only the solitary Goya of 1815 satisfies our imagination. Taine and Freud refute and exclude each other; does the self-portrait belong to Taine or Freud? "Analysis can tell us nothing about the elucidations of the artist's gifts, and the disclosure of the ways and means used by the artist in his work, the revelation of the artist's technique, also does not fall within the province of analysis."[6]

The portrait is a participle: to read it is to determine what it agrees with. The painter painting himself looks in a mirror at the model he constitutes and it is the mirror that he paints. The painter paints the viewer, the person looking at himself. When the mirror is eluded, the portrait looks at *me*. The portrait participle also agrees with this look that I give it, and through the interchange of looks *I participate* in the portrait itself. This reciprocity, a recurrence all too familiar in the museum gallery, initiates a confusion. Eluded, the mirror is still present, implicit, and through the looks exchanged, even if they are mutually irreducible, I become the other and the other becomes me. And this signifies that the self-portrait agrees with the fantastic.

Should we accept the spell it induces? If we refuse it, are we not denying the quality that makes the self-portrait impossible to reduce to any other genre? And isn't this deviation symmetrical with what had been the progress of the painter himself who had become the other of the portrait?

The portrait isn't its own commentary, just as the commentary can't be the portrait. Words like wrinkle, lip, lock of hair, chin, eyelid, nostril, eyebrow, corner of the lip, could not draw any face. Features described and portraits drawn *are totally unconnected*. A portrait implies that features and name agree with each other; there could be no portrait of the painter by himself if recognition were impossible. Names and features answer each other; identity is made up of a name if the name alone is not enough to establish it. But it is through a meticulous language, a repetitive, finical inventory, a tight description of the portrait, that the portrait can assume its meaning. What the portrait of the painter by himself reveals is the look itself; and what it reveals belongs to an entirely different sphere, that of narratives and anecdotes. In the same way as the reconstruction of a crime tells us nothing of the motive, a commentary on or inventory of a portrait remains powerless and can do nothing to penetrate the silence sealed within the painted lips of portraits.

As "narrative" or "anecdote," the portrait of the painter by himself cannot be the narrative only, the anecdote only. There is always an irreducible element that escapes. Is this because without room for doubt there can be no portrait of the painter by himself, or if not room for doubt itself, at least for unverifiable assumptions?

Raphael, who no doubt is "listening" to the discussion between Ptolemy and Zoroaster, is present, beside Sodoma, in the *School of Athens*. Filippino Lippi "witnesses" St. Peter's condemnation as Masaccio does his glory. Vasari, in the *Lives* of 1568, mentions eighty painters who are present in the frescos or altarpieces they painted. These painters are present in their works even if their presence is like that of Dante ("I know not, in truth, how I entered here...")[7] whom Virgil is guiding through hell in the *Divine Comedy*. What does this presence signify?

In the collection of self-portraits in the Uffizi Gallery, Florence, begun in the middle of the seventeenth century by Cardinal Leopoldo de' Medici, there are more than one thousand of them. And there is no museum that does not possess several self-portraits. The present account can be no more than an outline. No inventory could hope to be exhaustive and list all the portraits that all painters have left of themselves. In Henry Jouin's book alone, *Le Musée de Portraits d'Artistes* (Paris, 1888), more than two hundred self-portraits are mentioned. One day, perhaps, we should rewrite and extend this history of the self-portrait together with those produced by Charles-Adolphe Bonnegrace, Jean-François Donvé, Jean-Baptiste Tuby, Marie Yard, Baron Pierre-Narcisse Guérin, Jacques Autreau and Claude Hoin, to mention only French painters.

What follows is an endeavour to answer these questions as well as others that may arise. And the portraits mentioned are the replies themselves. The portraits are portraits of painters by painters; it is through these portraits that we shall be dealing with painters here. The text's only *raison d'être* is the pleasure of looking that these portraits afford; it is perhaps for this reason alone that the text may be said to have some connection with them.

Lastly, the following pages should not be taken as one of those demonstrations which offer proof and then stop. (This book is an art history book if we accept the definition of one given by Jacques Lacan: "The history of art, just like history and just like art, is a question not of the handle but of the sleeve, that's to say of a conjuring trick.") My aim is to define the self-portrait, more than as a genre, as a sign, in the manner one defines Pisces, Leo, Virgo or Gemini. (A precise hour determines trigons, quadratures and sextiles, and defines the astrological Houses, their importance and their relations in the way they cast their influence on the identity of a given person.)

The assumptions made, the connections highlighted, whatever is implied, understood or stressed, constitute the self-portrait's constellation. Together, these pages point to it.

This principle was the starting point for everything. The painter, as portrayed by himself, must not be reduced to a subject of history, but must be shown, by his pictured gaze, to be individual and timeless.

15

Filippino Lippi: *Self-Portrait, c. 1485*

Everything begins

Everything begins with a self-portrait sketch. Is this because it is unfinished? Still close to doubt. Uncertain. Imperfect.

The background is grey, buff, irregular. It is a smoothed coat of plaster, the saltpetre barely wiped off, and there stands a bust portrait. No text or sign other than this half-portrait cut off in the middle of the torso. The shoulders and the cap are roughed out. The features are brownish-beige touches; contours and seams.

The face is set off by collar and hair. The brown hair falls over the neck in strands and irregular curls. The loop of the ear stands out from the hair on the cap. At neck level we see the edge of the white shirt, which only just emerges from the closed collar of the jacket. Buttons, tips of a crushed paint-brush. The colour of this collar, covered on the left by that of the shirt, matches the hair.

Under the cap and hair, the forehead is low. The arches of the eyebrows are drawn irregularly. The eyes (a vague green?) open beneath heavy eyelids. The nose is broad, somewhat heavy. Teeth are visible between slightly parted, fleshy lips, painted a pale red. The chin, like the cheeks, is slightly thickened, but only faintly so.

The skin is smooth under the white lights and streaky shadows. No wrinkles on unevenness. The upper lip has a vertical groove; the chin is round, divided by a dimple in the middle. How old is he? About twenty. He has the good looks of youth. Nothing more.

In the gaze, a doubt is apparent. Something between calm and disquiet. Quizzical and almost grave. Tense. There is more assurance than arrogance. And prepared for withdrawal. And the look searches, engages the attention, defies. It describes, deciphers, decodes.

A similar attention (tension) of the slightly opened mouth, agape. Pausing. Expectant.

There is no ornament or accessory to distract the eye from this face encircled by dark hair. Nothing. Not even colour. The setting is neutral, devoid of architecture or landscape. This is nowhere. A banal cap, a banal shirt, banal... Neutral if not bare and stark. The face is alone. And the look on it dense, intense, is the only fact. What is it seeking?

Thus I am. Established fact. Am I thus? Established facts or questions are hypotheses. A drawing of solitude. I am alone.

What man begins here, the contrary of a might-have-been who resembles him?

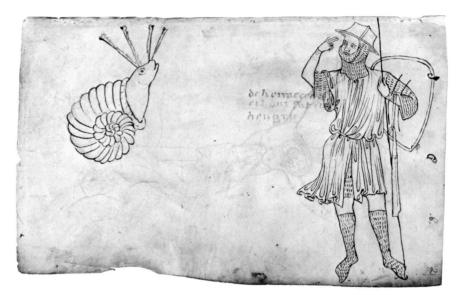

Villard de Honnecourt: *Self-Portrait, mid-13th century*

Nuns, monk, man-at-arms
or
The margins of writing

Among ground plans of churches and façade designs, in a book in which one may "find much counsel concerning the great strength of masonry and the engines of carpentry, the force of picturing and also the arts of geometry,"[1] there is the portrait drawing of a man-at-arms, wearing under his tunic a coat of mail. He has a helmet; in his left hand, a lance; and to the same arm are fastened a shield and sword. This armed man is Villard de Honnecourt, author of the book. Who is Villard de Honnecourt? Little is known about him. He travelled through Picardy, Champagne, Brie, and passed through Lausanne on the way to Hungary where, it would appear, he remained for some time. This was a long journey in the middle of the thirteenth century. The weapons do not imply that he was a soldier; at the time, such a journey could only be undertaken if one was armed. Is the "portrait" of Villard de Honnecourt by himself the signature of this manual?

About 1160-1170 at the Convent of Hohenburg, under the direction of Herrade, the mother superior, a *Hortus Deliciarum* (Garden of Delights) was written out and illuminated. Herrade, abbess by the grace of God, standing, presents the religious community. The same veiled face, repeated row after row, has the name of the nun written above it. Almost in the margin, alone and upright, Herrade

Herrade von Landsberg, Hortus Deliciarum: *Self-Portrait*
in the margin, c. 1160-1170

Guda, Book of Homilies: *Self-Portrait in an initial*
letter, 12th century

It was at the same period that Claricia, whose outspread hands appear to bear the illuminated orb of a letter, of which her curving body itself is a part, signs the page with her name and countersigns it by her presence. It was in the margin of a homily or a psalm that the portrait of the artist by himself appears by way of signature. And this portrait is only a portrait because it bears a name.

Herrade, Guda and Claricia were nuns; they have the same features and wear the same veils. But doubtless they had no mirrors in which to paint

Claricia: *Self-Portrait as the tail of a Q in*
a South German Psalter, c. 1200

offers the reader this Garden of Delights, a book to "delight the spirit by its honey." The veiled face of Herrade is similar to those of the other nuns of the convent. It is only a portrait of her because, like the other faces, it bears a name.

Standing within an ornamental letter, in the margin of a Book of Homilies, stretching out one hand, with its palm open, while the other holds the curving stem of the letter itself, is Guda. On this stem, beside her head, her name is written, and the rest of the text around her tells us that "a sinner she wrote and painted" this book. This drawing of a veiled nun is only a portrait because, without the least doubt, it bears a name. This is in the twelfth century.

Basso continuo

*Do you not know that there is
nothing in man more worthy of
contemplation than his face?*[1]

Apuleius

themselves in the convents of the twelfth and thirteenth centuries.

Matthew Paris, tonsured, kneeling and leaning forward with open hands extended under a framed Virgin and Child, proffers a text. In the margin of this Utrecht psalter which he copied, he tells us that he had been a scribe and painter. Further, he tells us that his glory as the "prince of scribes" will endure for ever.

In the margins of homilies, psalms and prayers began the history of the portrait of the "painter" by himself. Veiled nuns and tonsured monk are only portraits because they are near the names with which the work is signed. A portrait only exists when there is a name attached to it. And the portrait lays claim to glory and lays claim to it for ever. The signature it bears is a bid for fame and a challenge to death.

Matthew Paris, Historia Minor: *Virgin and Child with Self-Portrait, c. 1250*

Obstinately, ceaselessly, unrelentingly, we are dealing with a mirror, with its findings, confessions, truths and lies. The mirror is misleading. It is a place of interrogation: every mirror image is specious and suspect.

"Why in flat mirrors do images appear to be more or less equal to directly perceived objects?

"Why in convex and spherical mirrors are they smaller?

"Why, to the contrary, are they enlarged in concave mirrors?

"Why, in the latter also, are things that were on the left seen on the right, and inversely?

"In what conditions does an image withdraw to the interior of a mirror or project itself beyond the mirror itself?"[1] It is this same mirror questioned by Apuleius that painting seeks as a model. The mirror, then, becomes a criterion, a reference.

"Things copied from nature are amended by the mirror's judgment," says Alberti.[2] And Leonardo: "The painter's mind should be like a mirror which takes on the colours of objects and absorbs as many likenesses as there are before it. A mirror with a flat surface contains a true painting at its surface and a painting perfectly executed on the surface of flat material resembles the surface of a mirror."[3]

To paint himself, the painter proceeds through this mirror, which is a metaphor of painting. So to paint oneself is to paint painting itself; it is to paint both what is required and what is defined. To portray oneself, to paint a portrait of oneself, to "do" one's portrait, is to paint a mirror. ("To portray: to have oneself painted is no better way of putting it than to have oneself portrayed; so the majority of people say 'to have one's portrait done'.")[4] And this mirror trails myths behind it. These myths never cease to be present, just as a basso continuo is always present, muted but unceasing.

And to paint oneself is to reinvent painting anew each time. "I used to tell my friends what the poets' idea was: that Narcissus changed into a flower had been the inventor of painting; and, moreover, if painting is the flower of all art, the whole story of Narcissus is relevant here. Will you declare that painting is anything other than this manner of embracing – with art – this very surface of the spring?"[5] Alberti saw Narcissus as the inventor of painting. Now it was his face that Narcissus was gazing at on the surface of the spring. Each painter who looks at himself necessarily reinvents painting; this assumption underlies everything said here about self-portrayal.

Whether the mirror in which the painter looks at himself is a flat pool, polished metal or silvered glass matters little. It is always the mirror of Narcissus that is being painted.

Johannes de Eyck fuit hic

The Virgin seated on a throne holds on her right knee the child Jesus, naked and playing with a bird and a bunch of flowers his Mother is holding between the thumb and index finger of her left hand, angled towards her. The arms of this throne, standing in the apse of a church, are ornamented with sculptures: on the Virgin's right Cain is killing Abel, on her left Samson is cutting a lion's throat. Standing before this throne are a bishop and a knight; they are saints. No halo attests to their sanctity, only the text and their attributes identify them: SCS DONACIAN[U]S ARCHIEP[IS]C[OPUS] written below on the bevel of the frame, to the left, and the five-spoked wheel for St. Donatian, Bishop. Then, SCS GEORGIUS MILES XP[IST], written on the right for St. George, Knight. Apparently greeting the Virgin by raising his helmet, St. George stretches out his open left hand towards the Canon who, kneeling beside him at the foot of the steps to the throne, has paused in his contemplations of the Holy Scriptures. St. George is thus no doubt presenting this pious donor of the work itself to the Virgin and Child. The banner held by St. George rests against his left shoulder and is supported by the fold of his

arm; it is reflected in the upper part of the polished shield. It is the leather strap across the upper part of the saint's torso that retains this shield. Under this strap, practically in the shadows, we see on the polished metal a black form with red stockings, wearing a sort of red turban. This man is Jan van Eyck, painter, who signed the picture.

This reflection necessarily implies the painter's presence in the area of the apse. To St. Donatian's right, almost opposite St. George and Canon van der Paele, Jan van Eyck may well be observing the Virgin and Child.

"Johannes de Eyck fuit hic": St. George's shield vouches for that.

1. Jan van Eyck: *Detail from the Double Portrait of Giovanni Arnolfini and his Wife, 1434*

2. Jan van Eyck: *The Madonna of Canon van der Paele, 1436*

3. Jan van Eyck: *Detail of the Madonna of Canon van der Paele, 1436: The painter reflected in St. George's shield*

His eyes are in a wall
And their face is their heavy adornment.
One falsehood more by day,
One night more, and there are no blind
men left.[1]
Paul Eluard

Johannes Gumpp: *Self-Portrait, 1646*

The painter is portraying himself. Seated in front of his easel he is posing and painting. The canvas stands in front of him and gradually, stroke by stroke, features and a look are sketched in. This look scrutinizes him and amounts to a confrontation. The painter (this account is fictional) is seated and posing. On the left – is it placed on a table, hung on a wall, or standing on an easel? – is a mirror in which he observes himself. It is within the frame of this mirror beside him that he is posing. He views a painter seated in a room that he used as a studio and who is turning away from the canvas placed before him. This face he is looking at, is it that of a painter? Perhaps the mirror shows only this face and some of the chest, shoulders and torso, but neither palette nor paint-brush. The painter is looking at himself, but both palette and brushes are absent from the elements framed by the mirror. A face remains, a look remains; he is aware that they are his own. He knows that they are those of a painter; but there they are, unaccompanied by any attribute. The look he examines stares at him. And straightaway it is this look that accosts him: it is precise, incisive, relevant and immediate. Then the painter turns away to his right towards the canvas on the easel. He is viewing the same features which, uncertain, imperfect, are as yet only roughed out in chalk or perhaps charcoal; and these features, trait for trait, are those of the face he was examining a moment ago on his left. The look there is the same, a direct look, and now in the nearby mirror it turns away. He moves his paint-brush laden with colour closer to the pupil of the eye watching him under the eyelid that is as yet only a line lacking in thickness and weight. He paints this look exactly as he had just seen it in the mirror a moment ago. The painter paints this look that summons him; in reply, it seems to arraign him. He stares at it; he compels it to appear before him. This painted look is no vacant stare; it isn't the look of waiting that a pose held so often puts on a model's face. Like the contours of the roughed-out face, this look is a feature. Although this particular feature is quite different. It is not a description, it is not a line, it is a rough outline.

The look the painter is painting on the canvas is that of the painter in the act of looking; it is the look that only a few moments before was searching the mirror.

Stroke by stroke, the face becomes complete. The strands of hair and their shadows are arranged round the forehead and temples. The nose, the full lips, the arch of the eyebrows, a wrinkle, the chin, cast shadows on a temple, an eyelid, a cheek bone or the neck. The tone of the skin under the light, and the shadow true. The painter has painted this skin tone to resemble the one reflected by the tain of the mirror. (Tain and tone; equivocal homonyms, these words foreshadow a confusion which will not be the last.)

On the easel the portrait is finished. The painter looks at the portrait, at the mirror; at the portrait, at the mirror. Mirror and portrait are identical: the look and the disposition of the face in each are alike. Then, maybe, this labour complete, the painter gets up and returns to its usual place the mirror he has taken the time to paint. The portrait remains, an authentic copy, a surrogate for the mirror now removed. The portrait is a record of the mirror; ephemeral and mobile, the reflection is frozen, its fleeting moment caught. The painter looks at his portrait; a surrogate for the mirror, the portrait looks at the painter.

And (the fiction still continues here) painted in what was present time, the portrait watches the painter grow older. The portrait watches the face it once was become wrinkled with age. Indifferent, the portrait watches time, which from day to day discovers death.

The painter is dying.

The painter is dead.

The portrait alone remains, the last element of what was formerly this triangle in which the look, from reflection to reflection, from painter to mirror, from mirror to painter, from painter to canvas, the look resolves and discovers itself commonplace, inasmuch as it belongs in common to three paths: the painter's, the mirror's, the canvas's.

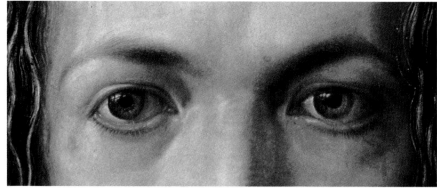

Albrecht Dürer: *Self-Portrait (detail), 1500*

I ("I" is the present reader) am looking at the canvas. I am looking at this other person whom I know to be a painter, who portrayed himself in . . . (I haven't yet read the copper plate, set in the frame, that gives the painter's name and the date of the picture), so I don't yet know when he did this self-portrait. I observe it: the face is handsome, plain, ugly. I consider the look in the eyes, and this look stares piercingly at me, catalogues me. This look from 1496, 1639, 1787, or 1849 (?) is present. I belong to a different period of time, and yet our eyes meet. We are looking at each other squarely, standing face to face. The moment created by these looks cannot be placed within any chronology, and acts as a delusion. What delusion is this "other" time? The eyes watching are the eyes in a painted mirror in which I am looking at myself. Back and forth from like to like go the looks, but like differs from like and this to and fro is a delusion. The satisfaction and dissatisfaction of a gaze are but one. Because this painted look that is a memory takes possession of my own look that it would have in oblivion, one or other of us must be the dupe. This is no longer Narcissus gazing at his reflection, but reflected eyes gazing at Narcissus.

A self-portrait: the painter looks out at us and his gaze challenges our own. He means it to be challenging; he means it to give us food for thought.

Jean-Auguste-Dominique Ingres:
Self-Portrait at the Age of Twenty-four (detail), 1804 and 1850?

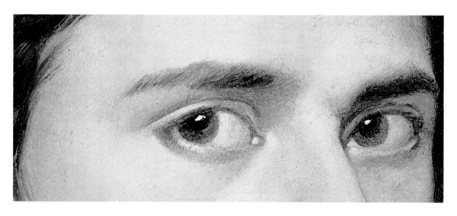

Epiphany

"About this time he also received an order for a small panel, to be placed in Santa Maria Novella, between the two doors of the main façade, as one enters by the middle door on the left. This panel is the *Adoration of the Magi*, with the old man in the foreground kissing the feet of Our Lord, overcome with emotion at having reached the goal of his long journey. This king represents Cosimo de' Medici the Elder: it is the most lifelike and natural portrait we have of him. The second king is Giuliano de' Medici, father of Pope Clement VII, who is piously paying homage to the Christ Child and offering him a gift. The third, also kneeling, who seems to be adoring Jesus and acknowledging Him as the true Messiah, is Giovanni, son of Cosimo. Beyond description is the beauty of all the figures whom Sandro painted in this picture, each one in a different attitude, seen either frontally, in profile, or in three-quarter view; inclined or in other poses, both young men and old, all of them treated with that variety which vouches for the perfection of his art. Since each king is represented by the attributes of his court, one can recognize to which king one or another retinue belongs. It is indeed so admirable a work by its colouring, drawing and composition, that any artist today would be dazzled by it. This picture gained him such a reputation in Florence, and elsewhere too, that Pope Sixtus IV, who had built a chapel in his palace in Rome, and wished to see it decorated, asked Sandro to take charge of the work."[1]

This picture illustrates the Gospel of St. Matthew: "When they had heard the king, they departed; and, lo, the star which they saw in the east, went before them, till it came and stood over where the young child was. When they saw the star, they rejoiced with exceeding great joy. And when they were come into the house, they saw the young child with Mary his mother, and fell down, and worshipped him: and when they had opened their treasures, they presented unto him gifts; gold, and frankincense, and myrrh."[2]

Only St. Matthew mentions this episode; John, Luke and Mark omit it. Who are these magi? Are they Persian astrologers? Are they heirs of Zoroaster, Prince of the Magi, priests of the pagan East? For a long time the Church mistrusted these magi whom Tertullian made into kings. They are three in number, an echo of the Trinity. They become the three continents of the world coming to the infant Christ: Europe, Asia and Africa. In the middle of the ninth century their names appear: Gaspar,

Sandro Botticelli:
The Adoration of the Magi, 1475-1478?

Melchior, and Balthazar, the latter first depicted as a black in the fourteenth century. They are the world kneeling before Christ. From the twelfth century on, they are also the three ages of life: Gaspar is the youngest, Melchior the oldest. Their very gifts become symbolic: gold is royalty, incense divinity, and myrrh, used for embalming corpses, indicates that the Son of Man's destiny is to suffer death for the redemption of all men. (For St. Bernard, matters are simpler and exclude these symbols: the gold will offset the Virgin's poverty; the incense will disinfect the stable; and the myrrh, an excellent vermifuge, will strengthen the child.)[3]

The identity of these three kings was discussed in Florence in the Confraternity of the Magi Kings, which was created in 1428 (and from 1446 the Confraternity arranged celebrations for the Epiphany). Discussions were held there, lectures given and canticles sung. Marsilio Ficino, no doubt, held forth before the devout humanists gathered there concerning his conception of these magi not as kings, but rather priests and philosophers; and their being called magi, or wise men, has nothing evil or doctrinally poisonous about it. Do they not belong to that Platonic theology which converts natural into supernatural knowledge? Opinions differ: Ficino sees them as possessing the wisdom of the Chaldeans; Pico della Mirandola as merely reflecting the inanity of pagan science.[4]

The Medici belonged to this Confraternity of the Magi Kings which held its meetings at the Convent of St. Mark. Lorenzo the Magnificent, like his father and grandfather, presided over this Confraternity, to which the Sacred College sometimes granted a year's indulgence for all its members. It was an *Adoration of the Magi* that Fra Angelico had painted on the walls of what was formerly Cosimo's cell in this Convent of St. Mark.

The fact that members of the Medici family belonged to the Confraternity is attested by Botticelli's *Adoration of the Magi*, which gathers together both the living and the dead. Of Cosimo, with grey hair, Vasari says that this is his "most lifelike and most natural portrait." Cosimo died in 1464; Giovanni, the youngest, died in 1463 at the age of thirty-nine; kneeling next to him is Piero the Gouty, who also died in 1463; Giuliano is standing behind Giovanni. Lorenzo stands on the left with his hands crossed on the pommel of a sword stuck into the ground between his boots. Upright, with his back to a partly collapsed wall, his hair turning grey, his index finger pointing, it would seem, towards himself, is the donor, Giovanni di Zanobi del Lama, a prominent money-changer and close friend of the Medici. And there in the foreground, a fair young man in a yellow toga, turning towards the viewer, is Sandro Botticelli – of whom Lorenzo the Magnificent was to say, in the lines of a burlesque poem, that he was "greedy as a fly."[5] It is true that his elder brother Giovanni had already been nicknamed "Botticella," the Little Cask, because of his plumpness, and perhaps this nickname was also applied to Sandro who was known as "the Glutton."

Among the figures in the retinues of the Medici magi, in this landscape of ruins, we find the painter.

Sandro Botticelli: *Self-Portrait (from The Adoration of the Magi, 1475-1478?)*

Above him, perched on the shattered wall, is a peacock: its outspread tail is the image of a starry sphere, and the eyes on its feathers were said to ward off the evil eye. The peacock's flesh, said by St. Augustine to be incorruptible, makes it the symbol of immortality. And its plumage, shed and renewed each spring, makes it the symbol of resurrection.

The peacock of immortality vertically above Botticelli is looking at the Virgin and Child. What immortality is Botticelli seeking by its position here? That of the soul no doubt; that of the work, possibly. His own presence signs the work and demonstrates that he has close relations with the Medici; it is both an established fact and an appeal.

Epiphany is a Greek word meaning "apparition." Perhaps this epiphany is also the apparition of the painter?

Albrecht Dürer: *Self-Portrait, 1498*

Albrecht Dürer: *Self-Portrait, 1500*

Pride and Humility
or
Because one is a Painter

To be a judge of beauty is to guess.[1]
Dürer

1498
Das malt Ich nach Meiner Gestalt...
Albertus Durerus Noricus...

On the left, the date 1500 above the monogram.
1498: the painter turns three-quarters towards the spectator. 1500: he is in front view. 1498: a lock of fair hair falls from right to left over his forehead, and in uneven curls his hair falls over his half-bare shoulders. 1500: a middle parting behind a tuft divides his hair which falls over the fur collar flaring out on the upper part of his chest and perhaps around his neck, hidden by the falling hair. 1498: Dürer is seated, or possibly standing, with his right forearm resting on a balustrade or table (?); in a room behind his right shoulder we see a column supporting the stone ribs of a vault. Behind A. D. an open window without a casing. It gives on a lake and mountain landscape. Beneath the window is a reddish hillock, and fields slope down towards the more distant lake. In the fields, the diminutive figure of a man at work. On the farther shore, the lake is bordered with trees, and then there are sharply rising slopes with abrupt spurs, passes and mountains. Snow covers the summits and the most distant slopes stretching to the horizon; the sky is blue, with floating clouds. The Alps, no doubt. But which Alps are these? Italian? German? Where precisely is Dürer? 1500: behind the painter is a uniform area of dark brown.

1498: Dürer is wearing a cap with black and white stripes; the front edge is folded back; a tassel of black and white fringes bound together hangs behind his right ear. His cape is held in place by a braided black and white cord, stretched horizontally across his upper chest which is bare above the Saracen-type shirt trimmed with gold. Over the shirt he wears a tunic, with black trimming, fastened at the waist; the shirt gathers into deeper folds at the point where the tunic buckle fastens. The right fore-sleeve is also trimmed with black. This sleeve is of the Italian type. The black pattern of the trimming cutting the slash at the elbow is evidence of this. The sleeve comprises several pieces, and may be of the kind that has to be sewn and unsewn every day when it is put on or taken off. The light-coloured gloves over the clasped hands are made of fine, flexible material. Dürer's elegance is that of a gentleman. 1500: he wears a dark fur-edged coat. His right hand is angled upwards and rests on the edge of the fur. And the gesture of this hand is similar to that of the Salvator Mundi.

1498: Dürer is a gentleman. 1500: Dürer is the Salvator Mundi. In 1498 as in 1500 the German or Latin inscriptions state that Dürer is both the painter and the model: ...*nach Meiner Gestalt* ... *ipsum me* ... A gentleman turning away, the Salvator Mundi facing us, in the same manner as the Dutch pictures of the "Vera Ikon" type, Dürer is in both cases a painter. Even more: it is because he is a painter that he can be like Christ.

From Venice Dürer wrote to Willibald Pirckheimer on the 18th of August 1506: "Here I am a gentleman." (By 1498 Dürer had already been to Italy, visiting Venice from the autumn of 1494 to the spring of 1495.) In Nuremberg he was unable to be this gentleman. On the 13th of October 1506 he wrote again to Pirckheimer: "You yourself write me how many prostitutes and how many respectable women ask of me. This is a sign of my virtue. But where you live you enjoy such consideration that you would never dare to converse publicly with a young painter; it would bring great shame upon you with so poor a painter." In Germany, being a painter still meant being a nobody; it was the Italian painters who were beginning to be intent on achieving fame. It was only during his first stay in Antwerp that Dürer was to receive the tokens of respect that he felt were due to him: "And when I was escorted to the table, people stood on both sides as if a great lord were being brought in. And among the people present there were also personalities much in the public eye who, with deep bows, all showed me the greatest respect." (*Journal*, 5th of August 1520)

No doubt he was not shown any such deference in Venice in 1494-1495. In 1506 the somewhat hostile reserve of the Venetian painters was unchanged, despite the appearance in 1498 of his "*Apocalypsis cum figuris*" which brought him exceptional fame as an engraver. He was an engraver, granted. Was he a painter? "I have silenced the painters: they said that I was a good engraver but that I lacked skill in the use of colour. Now everyone proclaims that he has never seen such beautiful colours."[2] Was it these alleged shortcomings as a colourist that were answered by the inscription on the portrait of 1500: "...*propriis sic effingebam coloribus*" (I portrayed myself thus in imperishable colours)? This portrait of 1500 only attests to one thing: Dürer's talent.

In the draft preface intended to open his book on the *Theory of Human Proportions*, Dürer writes: "The great art of painting has for many centuries been held in high esteem by the all-powerful. Indeed, they have enriched eminent artists and honoured them because they believed their talents to have been formed in the image of God. A good painter is truly filled with figures within himself, and were eternal life possible, he would always have something to impart to his work from his inner ideas, mentioned indeed by Plato." To be a painter is to be in the image of God; it is a life that imitates that of Jesus, and, further, it is the "Schola Crucis" of St. Augustine: "*Tota vita Christiani hominis, si secundum Evangelium vivat, crux est*" (The whole life of a Christian, if he lives according to the Gospels, is a cross). To paint oneself as a great lord is not vainglorious; to paint oneself as Christ is to paint oneself as a painter.

Digression concerning a parting in the middle

In 1843-1844 Friedrich Overbeck painted his own portrait for the Grand Duke of Tuscany. In it he wears a German cap. This old-style headdress is a proclamation of his patriotism. At that time to choose to be a German and a painter meant wearing that cap; equally it puts Dürer on a footing of equality with Raphael. And, in homage to Dürer, it meant drawing with a sharp-pointed pencil that practically engraves. Further, it involved arranging the hair with a parting in the middle, recalling that parting which, behind a tuft, divides Dürer's hair in his portrait as Christ of 1500. The cap (for Germany) worn by Overbeck no doubt conceals the middle parting that he suggests be worn (for Dürer). This impeccable middle parting is a feature of the self-portrait drawn in pencil in 1817 by Theodor von Rehbenitz.

This parting which, beginning with Dürer's, was meant to suggest a resemblance with Christ, earned the German painters who wore it the nickname of Nazarenes. The image of Christ traverses German patriotism in the age of romanticism.

Friedrich Overbeck:
Self-Portrait, c. 1843-1844

Theodor von Rehbenitz:
Self-Portrait, 1817

All the way to Calvary

His talent is "as if formed in the image of God."[1] Dürer does not doubt "because only a timorous intellect would be lacking in self-confidence to the point where it believed it could make no new discovery, but, to the contrary, follow the established paths and uniformly march behind others lacking the boldness to carry one's thinking beyond these limits. An enlightened intellect following another must not despair of finding something better with the passing of time."[2] Dürer's talent is a certainty and a self-commitment; and it is only a self-commitment because it is a certainty.

(Intended to be a Byzantine icon, in a variation of Dürer's portrait of 1500, Samuel Palmer paints himself as Christ. Living in solitude at Shoreham, in Kent, his mysticism had turned into fanaticism. The engravings of the blessed Bishop John Fisher and those of the man Fisher called his brother in martyrdom, Sir Thomas More, which Palmer wished to hang in his little chapel, were to help him to "rid my house and my heart of vice, levity and infidelity." Palmer as Christ prays.)

Prostrate, Christ affronts the bitter chalice of pain, solitude and death in the Garden of Olives. And this Christ is Gauguin. "The moments of doubt, the results always falling short of our dreams; and the lack of any real encouragement from others, all this is a thorn in our flesh."[3] Painting as the nineteenth century drew to a close had become a formidable commitment: "The painter's art calls for too great a body of knowledge. It requires of the artist a higher, dedicated life, especially when instead of going along with the general run he rises above it and becomes an Individual, having to take account of the peculiar nature of the creative artist, and to take account too of the surroundings in which he lives and his education."[4] The painter is alone: "In front of his easel, he is the slave neither of past or present, neither of nature or his neighbour. He contends with himself, only himself."[4] To make the painter's art express something, "it has got to be searched into unremittingly by searching into oneself."[4] In 1889 Gauguin is Christ in the Garden of Olives; he has a halo and is surrounded by apples and the serpent of Temptation; in 1896, near Golgotha, he is Christ once again. Let the brambles that pricked his flesh be woven together and they will become a crown of thorns.

Out of certainty and self-commitment, Dürer was Christ in 1500. Around 1890 it was for doubt and solitude that Gauguin was Christ.

Calvary has carried the day against glory.

Paul Gauguin:
*Self-Portrait as Christ
in the Garden of Olives, 1889*

Samuel Palmer: *Self-Portrait as Christ, c. 1833*

Raphael: *The School of Athens in the Stanza della Segnatura, 1508-1511*

Raphael: *Self-Portrait (centre) from The School of Athens*

Painters among philosophers and thinkers

People were debating, discussing, proving, demonstrating, annotating, exchanging views, arguing, reading, writing, and also listening and looking. Raphael's gaze goes beyond the bounds of the fresco. "Beside Zoroaster, Raphael painted himself with the help of a mirror. His head, covered by a black cap, is pleasant, graceful and delights us by its youth and modesty."[1] Close to him, on the right of the fresco is Sodoma: "As he was always surrounded by children and beardless youths, whom he liked beyond measure, he was nicknamed Sodoma; and, far from being angry, he boasted about it and composed on the subject couplets and triplets that he used to sing, accompanying himself on the lute."[1] Sodoma worked for Julius II in Rome, but too slowly for the Pope's taste and was dismissed.[1] "Then Bramante of Urbino, architect to Julius II, being related to Raphael and from the same town, wrote to him that, having spoken of him to the Pope, His Holiness had consented to employ him to paint the Vatican apartments... Being received with much kindness by Pope Julius, Raphael began work in the chamber of the Segnatura, where he depicted the reconciliation of Theology with Philosophy and Astrology [the so-called Disputa]. All the wise men of the world are gathered together here, arguing among themselves... So much did the Pope admire this masterpiece that he caused all the pictures by other painters in these rooms to be destroyed, so that Raphael should have the sole glory of replacing everything that had been done up to then."[1] The old frescoes of Piero della Francesca, Luca Signorelli and Bartolomeo della Gatta were thus destroyed, but not the vault, whose general arrangement, together with the cornices and some compartments, were by Sodoma. His presence at Raphael's side, in the *School of Athens*, vouches for the latter's appreciation of these paintings. Julius II wanted Raphael alone to have the glory of repainting the rooms; but Raphael associated Sodoma with his own glory.

On one side (in the *School of Athens*), the statue of Apollo the sun god, his lyre at his side, who seems to be trampling down the violence of brute force and sex embodied in the bas-reliefs beneath him, where naked men are fighting and a Triton carries off a Nereid, embracing her and squeezing her bare breasts. On the other side, the statue of Minerva, who seems to stand for clear thinking and intelligence. Opposed between them are Plato, with upraised forefinger, holding his *Timaeus* in his left hand, and Aristotle, stretching forth his open hand palm downwards and holding his *Ethics* against his hip. The higher reasoning of the Platonists is contrasted with the positive reasoning of the Aristotelians. Pythagoras is writing on the left. Opposite him with a compass is Euclid, bending down in front of Ptolemy, who is crowned and carries a sphere, in front of Zoroaster, who holds the terrestrial globe. Behind Pythagoras, on the left, are Averrhoes looking over his shoulder and Epicurus leaning against a column base and reading; beside him is Zeno, and at the top of the steps is Socrates talking with a group of men (is the one in armour Alcibiades or Alexander?), including Xenophon. Sitting alone on the lower step, his head propped on his hand, is Heraclitus, nearly in the centre. Assembled then in these rooms designed by Bramante (according to Vasari) are Grammar, Arithmetic, Music, Geometry and Astronomy. Plato is said to be a portrait of Leonardo, and Heraclitus of Michelangelo. By these portraits, as well as Sodoma's and his own, Raphael made Painting one of the Liberal Arts which till then had been refused by the hierarchy.

Raphael as painter is the peer of the thinkers and philosophers here assembled.

Hypothesis for an etymology and the play on words that comes of it

The portrait of the painter by himself is specular. Through the mirror the painter paints himself.

Speculum, like mirror – what does it matter if the word is Latin or not? – did not belong to the painter's vocabulary at the time when painters began painting themselves. This word belonged at first to the language of moral science. Encyclopedias and edifying tracts had such titles as *Speculum mundi, Speculum doctrinale* or *Speculum morale*. These particular mirrors offered examples of perfection to be striven for.

A mirror is a model.

Marguerite de Navarre wrote a *Mirror of the Sinful Soul* dealing with penitence, edification and devotional exercises. Benoît de Sainte-Maure in his *Romance of Troy* calls Helen "the mirror of all women": her beauty, that is, was the model for all beauty. Griseldis, for her patience and virtue, approaching those of Penelope, was called "the mirror of married women."[1]

The painter paints himself, using a mirror. *Speculum*, mirror. *Speculum*, to speculate, speculation. Philosophers, thinkers and poets speculate. Studies, theories and theorems are speculations. Speculation defines the Liberal Arts: Grammar, Arithmetic, Music, Geometry, Astronomy. The painter has no muse: neither Clio, nor Urania, nor Melpomene, nor Thalia, nor Terpsichore, nor Calliope, nor Erato, nor Polyhymnia, nor Euterpe had anything to do with painting. Mnemosyne, memory, their mother, forgot painting. The painter is a museless orphan who by including his specular portrait countersigns his fresco or altarpiece. At that time he began to lay claim to a higher status in the world.

Agreement of tenses and play on words: the portrait of the painter by himself appears when the painter claims to belong to the Liberal Arts. His speculation develops by way of the mirror.

"We only have recourse to what is called reflection because knowledge escapes us; forgetfulness is the flight of knowledge, and reflection, by awakening a new memory in the place of the departing one, maintains knowledge in such a manner that it appears to be the same."[2] Whoever paints himself using a mirror similarly rejects forgetfulness. Another reflection.

On earth as in heaven

Massacres, murders, martyrdoms, tortures, torments. Bodies are bound, bodies are empaled on lances, bushes, or sharpened branches, they are hurled from cliffs, they are stoned, lashed and flagellated, decapitated and amputated. These are bodies rent, crushed, stripped for death, and death is slow or violent.

A severed head, the eyes open and staring upwards, the tongue hanging out of the mouth, lies in a pool of blood on the shoulder of a toppled-over torso. A scimitar is about to lop off the blindfolded head of a kneeling man, naked, his waist girt by a knotted cloth, his hands tied behind his back. A great stone is about to crush the face of a boy, lying naked in a pool of blood, with his head upon the thigh of a nude decapitated body beside him. A shirt is rent from the shoulder and torso of another, his knee already bent with pain behind a crowned Christ standing upright before a cross of squared-off wood, still on the ground, in the midst of the tools, pincers and a drill, between two crosses of rough tree-trunks from which are hanging two crucified thieves, tied by the arms, one wearing a shirt and crowned with thorns, the other naked – a retold crucifixion, derisory and absurd, no doubt intended as such by Shapur and his henchmen in this valley lacking a Golgotha, where a fortified bridge can be seen across the river in the distance. And, in this presence, we also find the Gospels quoted: "And he that taketh not his cross, and followeth after me, is not worthy of me." [1] "Where I am, there shall also my servant be." [2] Each martyr put to death is Christ crucified, each martyr is a renewed calvary. On the right, a group of naked men bound together, held as if on a leash, are being whipped. They must climb those uneven stone and earthen steps which wind round an abrupt peak; they are preceded by another group partly hidden by the rocks. No doubt it is this path that leads to a sort of terrace from where armed soldiers are casting the bodies into space. A few soldiers who have remained below are finishing them off: one aims his lance at the falling bodies; another, on horseback, pierces the chest of a broken body with his, whilst another plunges his sword into the heart of a man whose head he pulls up by its grey hair. A fourth soldier is hacking off heads with an axe. At the foot of the peak skirted by the path, a soldier is using branches or rushes to whip men tied to broken tree-trunks; behind him, another is stoning a bearded old man who protects his head with a pitiful movement of his hands.

A black dog sniffs at the blood which flows in rivulets on the ground.

Shortly a sharp instrument will be used to pierce the eyes of Bishop Achatius who stands erect with his hands folded under his embroidered chasuble, wearing his mitre, and standing in the midst of a small group of men surrounded by soldiers. In a woodcut of ten years earlier the bishop, lying down in the foreground, is suffering the same torture. No doubt his presence was desired at the massacre of these ten thousand Christians, legionaries of Bithynia, ordered in 303 by Shapur, King of Persia, obeying the Edict of Diocletian. Shapur is depicted on the right on horseback, in the midst of his entourage and armed soldiers.

On the path from the river, running past the scenes of torture, are two men dressed in black, who, it seems, are indifferent to the massacre going on around them. They have halted in the centre between the group encircling the bishop and the procession to their left making its way towards the cliff to be put to death there. Neither of these two men looks at anything at all: neither the group itself between the cross of one of the thieves nor Shapur on horseback, where the decapitation, slaughter

Albrecht Dürer: *Self-Portrait (right),*
probably with Conrad Celtis
(from The Martyrdom of the Ten Thousand, 1508)

Albrecht Dürer: *The Martyrdom of the Ten Thousand, 1508*

Albrecht Dürer: *The Adoration of the Trinity, 1511*

and beating is in progress, although this fills up the area in the foreground. Similarly, not a single one of the tortured, not a single torturer, looks at these men. Their space-time continuum is not the same.

One of these two men – all in black, wearing a black headdress, with his long fair hair falling over his shoulders – holds in his folded hands a thin, nearly vertical stick which rests against the hollow of his left elbow. An unfolded paper seems to be caught in the slit pierced in the middle, on which I read: "*Iste fatiebat ano domini 1508/Albertus Dürer aleman*," and in the lower right corner of the paper sheet is the painter's monogram. And so this man wearing "a French-style coat purchased in Venice" is Albrecht Dürer. Probably the other man is Conrad Celtis, a friend of the painter and of the Elector who ordered the picture. (Celtis' gesture of intercession is a dual one: the humanist was perhaps giving the painter a few precise details – hence the changes that have been made in this painted martyrdom compared with the woodcut of ten years earlier – or it may be that the humanist was the go-between between Frederick the Wise and Albrecht Dürer the German painter.) The movement of the outstretched left hand, with the palm upwards towards the sky, is a presentation of both

the massacres and of the picture. Dürer, beside him, signs it; he signs it with his name, and proclaims that he is "aleman" (German) on his return from Italy; he signs it with his monogram, and he signs it with his features. The writing like the face is a conjunction of features. Another feature is the look aimed outside the painted space, with ourselves as the target. Their gazes summon our gaze, and by Celtis' gesture we turn our attention to the painted massacre. Similarly on the sheet of paper held up one word is isolated from the remainder of the text by the thickness of the wooden stick: "*Iste*," This. Celtis' gesture and Dürer's text add to each other, like their gazes.

The way they regard the murders with indifference suits us.

Today we view these men of 1508 who are showing us these ten thousand Christians martyred in 303. Their indifferent gazes are a denial of time. These gazes, and our gaze exchanged with them, alone remain and are contemporary. Time is nothing more than the time needed for this interchange of looks.

And their gazes and Dürer's gaze are something we need: it is they who introduce us to the martyrdom.

On the right, our right, of a landscape where the sparsely wooded rolling hills with a few scattered trees round a lake on whose shore a town can be seen far off, is Albrecht Dürer, standing, and holding an upright panel with his right hand. He wears a red beret from which his hair falls over the fur collar of his capacious coat. On the panel is the following inscription:

ALBERTUS . DURER
NORICUS . FACIE .
BAT . ANNO . A. VIR
GINIS . PARTU
1511

The painter's monogram is to be found on the lower right, on a level with the date.

The heavens open and extend above the landscape of this altarpiece painted for the Hallerheiligen Kapelle (All Saints Chapel) of the Nuremberg Zwölfbruderhaus founded by Matthäus Landauer and Erasmus Schiltkrot. Matthäus Landauer, who since 1510 had been living in this hospice, is guided into the procession of the faithful on the left by a cardinal, who turns round towards this white-haired old man. Above this procession joined by the donor, a Church procession guided by two Popes crowned with tiaras, the Virgin leads the files of saints and martyrs: St. Agnes and St. Catherine bear the attributes of their martyrdom in addition to the palm branches carried by each woman in this procession. Opposite the Virgin, St. John the Baptist leads the prophets, among them Moses with the Tablets of the Law and David with crown and lyre, followed by prophetesses and sibyls. Perpendicularly below this procession we find an emperor wearing on his chest the chain of the Order of the Golden Fleece, and a king; behind them is a crowd of laymen, ladies, soldiers and peasants. In the centre of the heavens, in the V of a cloud separating additional processions of saints and prophets, is the Holy Trinity: the Holy Ghost, a dove with outspread wings, hovers motionless above God the Father, shown as an emperor seated on a rainbow and surrounded by angels carrying the instruments of the Passion and holding open the ample green-lined chasuble against which the Son is crucified. This "City of God" is not yet that which the Last Judgment will initiate. God has not yet passed judgment. The "Celestial Court" and the "Christian community" cannot yet merge. The "*civitas dei*" founded by Abel and governed by Christ is not separated from the dregs of the "*civitas terrena*" founded by Cain and left to the Devil. It is this doctrine of St. Augustine that Dürer paints. Dürer is on earth living on a scale which is not that of this celestial city; Dürer, beneath this eternity, lives in the time-scale of mankind. The picture is dated A VIRGINIS PARTU, and here no "*Iste*" in the text points to these open heavens. The gaze of Dürer, a man, is that of the painter directed at those, also men, who are looking at this altarpiece on which is painted the City of God awaiting the Last Judgment. Dürer does not intercede; he does not introduce us to anything.

One credo alone is fitting; one credo alone is awaited. The same as his.

By his look Dürer intercedes for a narrative, not for a credo.

Albrecht Dürer: *Self-Portrait with upright panel (from The Adoration of the Trinity, 1511)*

Abyss

The mirror is the symbol of the Saviour
The mirror is the symbol of the Holy Scriptures
The mirror is the symbol of the Word Eternal
The mirror is the symbol of the life of Christ
The mirror is the symbol of Reason discovering God

The mirror is the symbol . . . It symbolizes many things for St. Gregory of Nyssa, St. Gregory the Pope, St. Bernard, St. Bonaventure, St. Lawrence Justinianus patriarch, for Raphael Mirami and Martin del Rio. Its many symbols are listed by Cesi under the title *De speculorum symbolis* in his *Mineralogia sive Naturalis philosophiae thesauri*.[1]

St. Paul the Apostle in his epistles to the Corinthians speaks of the mirror by which we shall be enabled to see God: "But we all, with open face beholding as in a glass the glory of the Lord . . ."[2] The theology that was founded on the New Testament was not the only one to look to the mirror as the place of the divine presence. Moses when returning from Sinai was unaware that his very countenance had become shining, as witness to the nature of the presence of Jehovah for forty days and forty nights.

Beyond the New Testament and the Old Testament, the mirror reveals the eternity and the image of the invisible God who is no longer the Helios of Olympus: "God has set in the heavens a most beautiful image of what he is, namely the Sun, which is the representation given by a mirror to those able to contemplate it by this intermediary."[3] (Is it chance that this mirror can not be looked at directly?)

God and the mirror . . . The mirror is a matter of theology, of cosmogony. The creation of the world by the Olympians was also brought about by the mirror, according to Proclus, a Neo-Platonic philosopher of the fifth century A. D.: Dionysus looked at himself in a mirror fashioned by Hephaestus; his own reflection captivated him, and from then on he created everything in his own image.[4] Dionysus is the only Olympian god who was born of a mortal mother, Semele. His father was Zeus. Dionysus is the wine god and it is because of this that he is dual: he exists outside man, and within man; he can transform him, making man resemble him. And this continually pruned god, tortured every year, who is no more than a vinestock, a knotty sawn-off branch (Dionysus is the only god who suffers), each year returns to life with the coming of the new spring. The Eleusinian Mysteries deal with this mystery too: the vine branches that have appeared again are a proof that the soul is immortal. Dionysus became a creator during the period when Greece had long sunk into decadence – Dionysus the tortured god who dies, and who each year, when spring recommences, returns to life to reaffirm the immortality of the soul. Dionysus, son of a god and a mortal woman, a child god who is confused with Protogonos, sometimes called Phanes, whose power embraces both the one and the many and cancels out the distance between the gods and men; Dionysus thus creates the world in his image . . .

"God created man in His Image and Likeness. Because of Original Sin, man lost the likeness and only retained the image," wrote St. Bernard of Clairvaux in his *De gratia et libero arbitrio*.[5]

The original sin that Adam committed was, according to the Gnostics, to look at himself and to love his own image.

Mirrors are abysses: for the impenetrable mystery of God and for the fall of mankind.

Attribute

The mirror is an attribute.

An attribute of Sight: "Its symbol is a young man holding a vulture in his right hand (because it was this bird that the Egyptians attributed to him according to Horapollo) and in his left a mirror, with a rainbow behind. The mirror indicates that this illustrious quality of sight is nothing other than something borrowed by our eye, which shines like a mirror or is limpid like water, from the visible forms of natural bodies, which sight perceives mirror-like, in order to communicate it to the senses and from the senses to the imagination, although the results are often false."[1]

And the mirror, again, is the attribute of Prudence because, "in order to govern his actions, the Prudent man examines his defects, something he cannot do without self-knowledge."[1] Let this knowledge become complacency, then the mirror passes from the hands of Prudence to those of Pride and Vanity. If it becomes a sign of pleasure enjoyed, Lust makes off with it. But if it does not lie, if it reflects things as they are, if it is only the repetition of fact, then it will be the attribute of Truth.

The mirror is the attribute of Lust, and also of Truth, or Pride and Vanity, but also of Prudence: it is an attribute of Sight. Contradictory, irreconcilable Virtues. The mirror, of itself indifferent, loses its neutrality through the look focused upon it; the look creates it.

("I have bought a mirror good enough to enable me to work on myself from it,"[2] wrote Vincent van Gogh to his brother Theo. Is this mirror that of Sight, Pride, Prudence, Vanity or Truth? Is it something different?)

Medusa

At that time there began the depiction of base subjects, a striving for coarseness and for the deformities that some persons continue to produce.[1]   G. P. Bellori

A Gorgon is shrieking, her mouth gapes open to utter a mute impossible scream. Her brow creases into furrows of horror. The vipers that are her locks, their heads darting, entwine, the strands knotted and venomous nip and bite each other, and their

Caravaggio: *Head of the Medusa, 1596-1598?*

tongues stretch out like pointed daggers. One of them, stringy, outlined like a scar on the severed neck below the lobe of the right ear, is reaching out for the spouting blood. The eyes, all sleep swept away by pain, are watching. Is their gaze not turned to the headless corpse stretched out on the ground, already decomposing and washed by a pool of blood round the shoulders? Blood pours from the severed arteries and veins in a spurting jet. The head will tumble to the ground in death. The murderous blow only just struck, Medusa is already in the arms of death. And Perseus in his polished shield surveys the reflection of this frightful head.

"Through secret places, hidden from every eye, inaccessible and remote, across rocks where thorny forests thrive, I reach the dwelling-place of the Gorgons. Here and there on field and path I had perceived the bodies of men and animals which, having lost their original shape, had been turned into stone at the sight of Medusa. But I looked only at the reflection of her hideous countenance in the bronze of the shield clasped in my left hand, and when she and her snakes had sunk into a deep sleep, I struck off her head from her neck."[2]

The mirror is a murder weapon which staves off death. To look at Medusa is to die. The inverted reflection of the odious and mortal head of Medusa is alone visible. Medusa's portrait can only be a painting of this reflection. The portrait of Medusa presupposes a mirror and here it is an essential mirror that has been painted. We are Perseus. Our place is that of the assassin.

And Medusa is Caravaggio: the portrait of the Gorgon is the portrait of the painter by himself. The painter like Medusa arrests, kills; painting is said to be a form of murder or crime. To paint is to kill. Because painting negates time, because it arrests a gesture, a look, an attitude, it kills. Time rejected is death. And every painter is Medusa.

To be Medusa is death denied. Medusa is the only mortal Gorgon, but the severed head of the dead Medusa does not cease to kill. "Fearing that the hard gravel might wound the head crowned with serpents, he lays out on the ground some tender foliage, piles up a layer of delicate stalks which had grown under water, and sets down there the head of Medusa, daughter of Phorcys. Contact with the monstrous head and these freshly cut stalks which had still been kept alive by their spongy core show the effect in a trice: they solidify! Reeds and foliage are now rigid as never before."[2] Polydectes and his assembled guests all perished because for one instant they had glimpsed the severed head that Perseus brandished, his face averted, his fist grasping the snake hair. Medusa, herself dead, kills; her dreadful head fastened to the shield is a weapon. It is not this shield that claims our eyes, it is not this shield adorned with these mortal remains that we are looking at.

When I look at the severed head, I hold out the mirror in which I am looking at the invisible. And Caravaggio is invisible. He, a man, is this woman who was beautiful. At Perseus' wedding to Andromeda he spoke of this: "Celebrated for her beauty, Medusa was courted by numerous suitors who contended for her jealously; there was nothing in her person as admirable as her hair: I knew someone who assured me that he had seen her. It is told how the god of the Sea dishonoured her in a temple of Minerva. Jupiter's daughter turned away, covering her chaste countenance with her shield and, so as not to leave such an outrage unpunished, she transformed the Gorgon's hair into frightful serpents."[2] Who is Caravaggio?

Medusa dead is immortal: her horror exercises death, her power after death is her presence.

To be Medusa is to deny death, and also to be nothing other than death; it is to be the one who dies and the one who goes on killing. This adolescent head lopped off is both death received and death given.

The mirror is the theatre of a murder, and Medusa is not watching her death in it, and Caravaggio, assassinated, is not looking at himself in it. Who then is the Perseus of Michelangelo Merisi known as Caravaggio? And it is his own death that Caravaggio paints: he does not paint himself as a mortal, but dead, dead of a violent death. This portrait is a posthumous portrait.

Who is Caravaggio?

"When thou wouldst know thyself and who thou art, look on the gravestones as thou journeyest by . . . Look thou on these and know thyself the man thou art."[3]

To pause and look on "these" is to face death. To face death is to know oneself. Another reflection. I learn for myself in the mirror what my death is. Who is Caravaggio? The mirror is knowledge. The mirror is the assassin. Mirrors open up an abyss.

Of Mercury, god, planet, and element called Hg or
The other side of the mirror

A mirror is a sheet of glass whose reverse side is silvered with tin and mercury.

Mercury, a handsome agile adolescent, is the son of Zeus and Maia, one of the Pleiades, the daughters of Atlas; he is the messenger of the gods.

Quicksilver takes its name from Mercury (and the name of this element is reduced to Hg), the name of the planet with which alchemic analogy associated it. For the alchemists the symbol of the metal was the planet itself.

Mercury, whose diameter is only slightly longer than the moon's, is the planet closest to the sun. Mercury requires no more than eighty-eight days to complete its revolution. This speed gives it its name: it is agile, just as the god is.

From the god of Olympus to the silvered metal on the reverse of the mirror, we derive a chain of metaphors and analogies, interwoven with a chain of age-old myth.

And Mercury is not indifferent to the looks directed at him, not indifferent to his myths. He plays with those looks, makes game of them.

It was to Argus, Argus of the hundred eyes, that Hera entrusted Io to be looked after. Io, daughter of Inachos, who was a virgin, having wandered long in search of love, was changed into a heifer by her lover Zeus to deceive the jealous Hera; but Hera was not duped and demanded that the heifer be a gift to her. Mercury outwitted this custodian who had the ability to sleep just closing two eyes at a time and continuing his vigil with those that remained open during his sleep. Mercury spoke in a lethargic and monotonous voice, interspersed by opiate passages of music from his pipes. And all the eyes of the dead Argus, those hundred eyes, Hera scattered on the peacock's tail.

Only the Graeae knew the way to reach the Gorgons and Perseus boasted at Polydectes' wedding that he had the power to kill one of the three: Medusa. Th Graeae, three grey, wizened hags, possessed only one eye between them, a single eye. In this place of shadows where they dwelt, one was doubtless enough. Mercury it was who counselled Perseus to steal their one and only eye just at the instant when one of them had taken it from her socket and was for the moment blind, while she was handing it to another, herself still sightless. Perseus should steal this eye at that very instant and keep it to use as blackmail: an eye in exchange for the route that would lead him to the Gorgons.

Mercury, through Perseus, once more deceives the eye.

The eye deceived is also a definition of painting.

Dosso Dossi: *Jupiter and Mercury, 1529?*

Apelles, Lord of Steen

*And, as he only gave up Painting
for business, he likewise only gave
up business for Painting, which
exercised the most powerful
fascination on his heart.*

Roger de Piles[1]

Bird's beaks crack on the seeds of the grapes painted by Zeuxis; Zeuxis' hand slips on the panel where he tries to grasp the folds of a garment painted by Parrhasios.

Mercury is a metaphor of painting; Mercury is illusion, trompe-l'œil – whether this eye is the single one of the Graeae or the hundred of Argus. Mercury is trompe-l'œil, the eye-deceiver.

Such is the messenger of the gods. He is not the only one at the gods' command: Iris is also their messenger. And Iris is the goddess of the rainbow; a rainbow which, as Aristotle explains, can only become visible in the multiple mirrors formed by rain-drops. It is through Iris that the refracted, diffracted light appears in colour.

Through the messengers of the gods, the eye's gaze becomes conjecture; Mercury is a trompe-l'œil; Iris creates spectral light. The silvered reverse of the mirror is the place of myths.

A mirror is a sheet of glass whose reverse side is silvered with mercury and tin.

Tin, in Latin *stannum* or *stagnum*. An odd coincidence: the word *stagnum* designates both the metal and standing water, water that is stagnating. Is this the still water where Entelidas, leaning forward, gazes at himself and cannot tear his gaze away, charmed by his own beauty, hypnotized by it until death takes him? Is this the water where Narcissus, handsome and uncaring, discovers that he is the subject of his own love, until then aimless? Is this stagnant water also the water of the Styx, where the dead Narcissus, ferried by Charon, still continues to gaze at himself?

On the reverse side of the mirror, silvered with tin and mercury, our etymologies, analogies, metaphors and symbols go to create myths in the depths of the abyss.

And Mercury becomes Sosia "by robbing him of his name and resemblance."[1] And Sosia, dispossessed, asks: "And, in short, canst thou contrive that I shall no longer be myself?"[1] "And can I cease to be myself?"[1] "But if thou art myself, tell me who it is thy wish that I should be. Because, for all that, it is certain that I must be something."[1]

The following words are carved on a memorial stone in a chapel of the St. James Church in Antwerp: NON SUI TANTUM SAECULI SED ET OMNIS AEVI APELLES DICI MERUIT. (He deserved to be called not only the Apelles of his time, but the Apelles of all time.[2]) Above this memorial stone where, since the first of June 1640, the mortal remains of Peter Paul Rubens lie, and above the altar, hangs a Rubens canvas: the *Virgin Surrounded by Saints*. Standing, in dark-coloured armour, holding his banner behind Mary Magdalene, who with bare breasts advances towards the Virgin, is St. George. This St. George is said to have Rubens' features, the Virgin those of Isabella Brant and Mary Magdalene those of Helena Fourment; these at any rate are the identifications handed down by tradition.[3] He who rests in this chapel is the Lord of Steen, Secretary of his Catholic Majesty in his Privy Council, knight of the Holy Ghost, and painter of the Cardinal Infanta. His coat of arms is as follows: A shield parted per fess, in chief or a horn sable and in cantons two cinquefoils pierced or, in base azure a fleur-de-lys or, helmet visor open, hatchments and tassels or and argent and for the crest fleur-de-lys or. When Rubens was knighted in 1630, the King of England added an augmentation: on a canton gules a leopard or.[4]

The tomb inscription simply describes him as Apelles and fails to mention the name Rubens; the Rubens painting chosen for the chapel shows St. George as a knight beside the Virgin.

Rubens a painter?

Rubens never at any time portrayed himself as a painter.

Peter Paul Rubens and Isabella Brant are posing at the foot of a tree. He sits on a stool. She is seated to his left on a lower stool or on the grass itself. Isabella Brant wears a hat with the brim partly turned up and lined with satin, over a cap which probably holds her hair dressed in a chignon above the light lace collar encircling her neck. The bodice is of black and white satin; at the front, the white satin embroidered with flowers tapers down to the violet skirt trimmed with gold. This no doubt is the dress she wore at their wedding in 1609. Rubens' left hand rests on the hilt of his sword and the elbow of this arm on a rung of the ladder behind them. He is equally elegant: lace, embroidery, ribbons, and

Peter Paul Rubens: *The Artist and his Wife Isabella Brant*
in the Honeysuckle Bower, 1609

2

Peter Paul Rubens:

1. *The Walk in the Garden (The Artist and his Second Wife Helena Fourment), 1630-1631?*

2. *Self-Portrait with Justus Lipsius, Jan Woverius and his Brother Philip Rubens, c. 1611-1612*

3. *Self-Portrait, 1637-1639?*

velvet. Isabella's hand lies on Rubens' half open one. Their life together is beginning. In 1626 Isabella died: "In truth I have lost an excellent companion; one might – what am I saying? – one certainly should cherish her for good reason because she had none of the faults of her sex, no moods of melancholy, no woman's foibles ... to the contrary, nothing but goodness and delicacy. Her virtues made everyone fond of her when she was alive and after her death they have caused universal regret."[5] In 1609, beside Isabella Brant, sits Rubens her husband. There is nothing in the portrait to tell us that he is a painter.

In the garden of his house Peter Paul Rubens and Helena Fourment are strolling, followed by Nicolas

Rubens, Isabella Brant's son. They are walking towards an Italian-style pavilion with columns and sculptures; on one side a woman is feeding grain to two peacocks and a turkey following; the grain swells the pocket of her apron that she holds up with her left hand. Further off, in the garden over the basin of a fountain, a dolphin spouts water. They have just passed a flower bed planted with tulips and enclosed by orange trees in pots. Perhaps they intend to sit a while in the pavilion for there are two chairs in readiness. Helena Fourment wears a straw hat ornamented with flowers, Rubens a black felt one. Helena's black dress, turned back at the skirts under the white apron, is lined with yellow. Rubens wears black. A widower, he has just taken Helena Fourment as his second wife. In the garden the group turns to look back at the dog who is probably about to frighten the birds. In 1630 or 1631 we see Rubens beside Helena Fourment. There is nothing in the picture to tell us that he is a painter.

Neither with Isabella Brant nor with Helena Fourment does Rubens portray himself as a painter.

Seated at a table in an interior, Justus Lipsius, wearing a fur-collared coat, is in all likelihood quoting some text to which he points with the index finger of his left hand; a book is lying open on the carpet of a table where we see pens as well as other books with thick bindings. On Lipsius' left, in profile, is Jan van den Wouwere, known as Woverius; beside him, a dog stretches out a paw. Opposite, wearing a stiff ruff, is Philip Rubens and behind him his brother Peter Paul Rubens is walking by and turns towards us. These learned men may well be discussing philosophy; behind them is a bust of Seneca in a niche, and closeby a vase with four tulips, of which two are already open. A landscape is visible beyond a column and a drawn-back curtain.

There is Rubens, with his brother and Woverius, listening to their master, Lipsius. There is nothing to indicate that he is a painter.

Peter Paul Rubens is alone. His gloveless hand rests on the hilt of his sword. The hat and coat he is wearing are both black. His face is set off by a white ruff.

"In 1628 the Courts of Spain and England were considering peace, and the Marquis of Spinola, who was very familiar with Rubens' merits, was of the view that no one was to be found who would make a better negotiator. He discussed the matter with the Infante, who approved of his choice and sent Rubens to the King of Spain with the express task of proposing ways and means for peace and to get instructions. The King was so pleased with him and judged him so worthy of the enterprise for which he had been sent, that he knighted him and gave him the post of Secretary of his Privy Council, whence he was directed to send letters for the King and his surviving son Albert . . . When Rubens had concluded the peace, meeting the wishes of the peoples and to the satisfaction of the two kings, he took leave of the Sovereign of England who, to show his recognition, prior to Rubens' departure, conferred upon him a knighthood just as the Catholic King

had done in Spain. To his coat of arms he added a canton charged with a leopard and in a session of parliament drew his sword so that he could present it to Rubens on whom he further bestowed a fine diamond that he removed from his own finger as well as other diamonds worth ten thousand crowns . . . The King of Spain, made him a Gentleman of the Bedchamber and honoured him with the Golden Key."[1]

This was Rubens.

This elegant young man sitting beside Isabella Brant, this gentleman accompanying Helena Fourment, this same gentleman together with his friends, this St. George appearing before the Virgin, is never seen as a painter.

And this knight of the Kings of Spain and England whom the King of Spain honoured with the Golden Key is not like the man he met in Madrid who painted a portrait of himself with a key at his waist: Don Diego Velázquez, Gentleman of the Bedchamber to the King of Spain. Peter Paul Rubens painted Peter Paul Rubens.

3

43

Paolo Uccello: *Bust Portraits of Giotto, Uccello, Donatello, Antonio Manetti, and Brunelleschi, 15th century*

In memoriam

"Paolo Uccello esteemed the talents of his colleagues and, in order that their memory might remain alive among generations to come, he depicted on a long panel five famous masters and kept it at home in their memory: one, Giotto, the painter, represented the beginnings of art; Filippo Brunelleschi, architecture; Donatello, sculpture; and himself as a painter of animals and perspective; in addition, for mathematics, his friend Antonio Manetti."[1] (In the first edition of his *Lives of the Painters*, Vasari attributed this row of head-and-shoulder portraits to Masaccio.) A mathematician, an architect and painters are shown together. Friendship and admiration unites them. These portraits are a tribute and have been painted so that posterity may keep alive the memory of what these men were. This is a considered record of their features, so that memory will be able to connect a man's face with what he knows to be the work of each. (These portraits have ensnared time: through them these men are present in the memory.) Here there must be a name. These features require it, demand it. To recognize is to put a name to a face. The features of the handwriting of a name cover those of a face. This face in three-quarter view with a round cap; this face with its forehead scored by symmetrical wrinkles curving down to the right side of the nose; this face partly framed by a white beard of which the pointed ends divide on the chest; this face is that of Paolo Uccello. And it is only Paolo Uccello because his own name is written beneath like underscoring.

A portrait is a confession of its own inadequacy; its deficiency lies in its silence. It is still Harpocrates, the god with his index finger held up to closed lips, who is silent and who imposes silence; implicitly all portraits stem from him.

To paint a portrait *in memoriam* for that brand of immortality known as posterity, is to paint a named face. Salvation, be it death denied, civility or respect, requires a name. To paint oneself for a posterity enjoined to identify the portrait is to impose silence on Harpocrates himself by a few written words, and the requisite writing is a confession of one of painting's limitations.

(Fastened to a frame is an engraved plate of copper or plastic that announces: Portrait of a Man. [What does the painter's name and the date of this particular portrait matter?] Portrait of a Man. Portrait of whom? Portrait of whom in – here the date – was painted by – here the artist's name. Portrait of no one. Another dead figure out of the past.

These portraits of Manetti, Brunelleschi, Donatello, Giotto and Uccello, these portraits of artists assembled by Uccello, remind us that he was not the first to bring artists together in this way. This theme was initiated by the portrait of the Gaddi. Here we have three faces: one in three-quarter view, the next facing us and the third in profile. Above the heads in roman script are the names: TADDEVS GHADDI GADDVS ZENOBII ANGELVS TADDEI

Agnolo Gaddi: *Self-Portrait (right) with portraits of Taddeo Gaddi and Gaddo Gaddi, 1380?*

Max Ernst: *All Friends Together, 1922*

More than five centuries have passed.

Two sheets of red-backed paper hang like scrolls, one on either side of a group of men and a woman gathered together in a mountain landscape of crags and clouds. Some, in the front row, are seated on non-existent chairs, others are running or dancing around the rock-ledge platform.

On the left-hand sheet is written:

1 René Crevel
2 Philippe Soupault
3 Arp
4 Max Ernst
5 Max Morise
6 Fédor Dostoiewski
7 Rafaele Sanzio
8 Théodore Fraenkel
9 Paul Eluard
10 Jean Paulhan

On the right-hand sheet:

11 Benjamin Péret
12 Louis Aragon
13 André Breton
14 Baargeld
15 Giorgio di Chirico
16 Gala Eluard
17 Robert Desnos
December
1922

and in the lower right corner of this latter sheet: Max Ernst. This signature repeats on the right sheet the name listed as No. 4 on the left sheet.

The figure 4 is painted in the hollow of the neck of a man who is young despite his white parted hair; he is wearing a dark green suit with the coat severely buttoned over a tie and white shirt. This man sitting on Dostoyevsky's leg (he has the figure 6 painted on his beard) is Max Ernst.

Writers, poets and painters are gathered on this rock ledge which serves as their meeting-place. Beside each of the faces an arabic numeral is painted; two lists, painted on scrolls unfolding in mid-air, show the correspondence between these figures and names, among them the painter's own. Faces keyed with figures, in the same way that linen is embroidered with initials; lists that decipher.

(If such a punctuation mark existed, here would open what I should call a prudential parenthesis. The painted hands in this group portrait of *All Friends Together* are curious. Fingers parted in a specific, telltale manner, palms angled to varying degrees. These gestures are those of the deaf and dumb language. Here a voluble Harpocrates is invented; the index finger sealing the closed lips with silence moves, and through some grammar of attitudes and figures, speaks. Gesture becomes speech. For centuries, for the painted speaker, the gestures of talk have been repeated wordlessly; with Max Ernst, silent painting ceases to be wordless.

Rembrandt: *Self-Portrait with Saskia*
or The Prodigal Son, c. 1635.

Who is laughing?

"If you take the great late
self-portraits of Rembrandt,
you will find that the whole
contour of the face changes time
after time; it's a totally different
face, although it has what is called
a look of Rembrandt, and by this
difference it involves you in
different areas of feeling." [1]

Francis Bacon

"The only saying of Rembrandt's
that we know is this:
I have never painted anything
but portraits." [2]

Henri Matisse

Rembrandt turns round, with his left hand in the small of Saskia's back as she sits on his knee, and laughs. This is a picture of 1635. In another he has a slight stoop (is it age? is it mirth?) as he stands in front of a portrait bust on a level with his cap. He is laughing. This is a picture of 1665. Thirty years lie between these two laughs.

Who is laughing?

1635. Rembrandt is seated in front of a table. Saskia, seen from behind, sits on his lap. Both are wearing clothes of velvet and silk, and chains, and his beret is of dark-coloured velvet with light feathers; a rapier stuck in his cross-belt makes an oblique line down to his calf. In his raised right hand Rembrandt holds a tall beer glass: most likely he is drinking to the health of the picture's spectator, at whom both he and Saskia have turned to look. We imagine that in a moment they will both turn back again to the table, covered as it is with an oriental carpet and set with dishes: a pie has as its cover a peacock, no doubt sewn together again. Who knows, behind Saskia there may be jars of wine and more dishes of food for this feast started off with an unfurled peacock's tail in the background. On the left, hanging on the wall is a framed slate. And Rembrandt, with his left hand on Saskia's hip, almost her buttock, as she sits on his knee, is laughing.

Rembrandt is not Rembrandt, Saskia is not Saskia.

At an inn lying a few leagues from his father's house, a prodigal young man who has just been paid his share of his inheritance is starting on a feast, after which he will spend the night in the bed of the prostitute seated on his knee. The following morning, stripped of everything, this young prodigal will be driven away by the innkeeper and the girls. Such scenes with their debauchery and the next morning's imagined come-down were frequently depicted in Holland during these early years of the seventeenth century. "The Prodigal Son" was a theme that sold well. This foolish prodigality was perhaps

46

a moral lesson suited to the economic expansion then getting under way. It was on the slate hanging on the wall that everything the client consumed was chalked up. And the peacock's open tail set on the table was the symbol of pride and sensual pleasure.

This picture is not a portrait of the painter by himself with his young wife; it is a scene from the Gospel according to St. Luke: "A certain man had two sons: And the younger of them said to his father, Father, give me the portion of goods that falleth to me. And he divided unto them his living. And not many days after the younger son gathered all together, and took his journey into a far country, and there wasted his substance with riotous living."[3] This young man seated in a tavern is not called Rembrandt. The prodigal son is laughing.

1665. In four years Rembrandt will be dead, and Rembrandt is laughing. Was he laughing over his life and its events? Was this laugh saying that life was nothing but vanity, with the births and deaths of four of his children and Saskia's death, and glory and fortune and failure, and Hendrickje's death? Was Rembrandt's laugh a challenge to all that? Rembrandt was taking his last steps and the road along which he had journeyed was posted with a final milestone; on it a Hermes. We may ask if this Hermes was the profile in the semi-darkness behind the painter. But can Hermes have this wrinkled face with the loose flesh under the chin? The hypothesis is uncertain. Rembrandt is laughing. Is he meant to represent Democritus? Democritus of whom legend ignores the fact that he imagined the world as made up of indivisible and indestructible atoms moving about in the void. Democritus of whom legend made the laughing philosopher. The personage behind him, wrinkled, cantankerous and sombre, would then be Heraclitus, his opposite. But can Rembrandt be this laughing philosopher, when he constantly underlines the fact that he is a painter; a painter identified by the chain worn round his neck, that chain by which Cesare Ripa says that painting clings to resemblance, to nature imitation; and a painter because of the maulstick he holds before him obliquely. Why then make of Democritus a painter? A doubtful assumption. Rembrandt, a painter, is laughing. Whose wrinkled face is this in the semi-darkness behind him?

In London, in 1761, were published the six volumes of a guide to the wonders of the city and its outskirts. In it, one Sampson Gildony was said to have in his collection a canvas described as "Rembrandt painting an old woman, by himself." This is the same subject that Aert de Gelder, Rembrandt's last pupil, painted in 1685. An old woman is posing; she holds an apple in her hand; this wizened old woman has commissioned a portrait of Venus from the painter and wants to be the model. This anecdote is well known to all painters. Of the dictionary *De verborum significatione* by Marcus Verrius Flacus, all that remains are the extracts copied by Sextus Pompeius Festus. Under P for Pictor we find: "Pictor Zeuxis risu mortuus, dum ridet effuse pictam a se anum."

This old man leaning over in front of a canvas is not called Rembrandt. Zeuxis is laughing.

Rembrandt: *Laughing Self-Portrait, c. 1665-1668*

"Festus says that Zeuxis' last picture was the portrait of an old woman, and that this work so much amused him that he died in a fit of laughter. Although the matter is hard to believe, it is not unexampled."[4]

In 1635 Rembrandt painted the *Prodigal Son*. He is the model for it.

In 1665 Rembrandt painted Zeuxis. He is the model for it.

Possibly these two portraits were painted with a connected purpose behind them. The first may be an exorcism: painting oneself as a prodigal and rake so as not to become one. The second may be a challenge: painting oneself as a mythical painter in order to become one after death.

Hinrik Bornemann the Younger:
*St. Luke painting the Virgin
(with self-portrait lower right), 1499*

St. Luke

*The symbol of St. Luke, patron
saint of painters, is, as you are
aware, an ox. So you must be as
patient as an ox if you wish to
work in the artistic field. But
bulls are very lucky not to have to
work with dirty paint.*[1]

Van Gogh

Pierre Mignard:
*St. Luke painting the Virgin
(with self-portrait, left background,
holding palette and brushes), 1695*

James Ensor: *The Virgin as Comforter, 1892, with self-portrait as St. Luke*

The fifteenth century is drawing to a close and Bornemann, at St. Luke's feet, implores the viewer of the altarpiece for his prayers. The seventeenth century is drawing to a close and Mignard, soon to die, standing behind St. Luke, is watching the Saint putting the finishing touches to the portrait of the Virgin. The nineteenth century is drawing to a close and Ensor, self-portrayed as St. Luke kneeling, offers the standing Virgin who holds a palm and a lily, the portrait he had made of her whilst she was suckling the Child Jesus.

From century to century, St. Luke. He is the patron saint of painters. Guilds and academies throughout Europe invoke the Evangelist's aid, as sculptors invoke the aid of the four crowned martyrs, Claudius, Castorius, Symphorianus and Nicostratus, who in the reign of Diocletian were whipped, then shut up in coffins that were sealed with lead and thrown into the water, all because they refused to carve an Aesculapius.[2] St. Luke, or so a text records, painted the portrait of the Virgin. Hence his traditional position as patron.

Apelles and St. Luke reinforce each other. These two painters' standing with posterity is based on such absent works as the portrait of Alexander which made Bucephalus neigh and the portrait of the Virgin who posed with the Christchild. (But painting, if done by Apelles or done by St. Luke, differs: it is desire or prayer. Prayer is the portrait done by St. Luke. Campaspe, Alexander's mistress, posed for Apelles; and Alexander offered Campaspe to Apelles who could not hide his desire for her. It is not immaterial that painting can be a metaphor both of prayer and of desire, that its model can be either the Virgin or the courtesan.)

It is the Holy Ghost, a dove with wings spread before its breast, who dictates to Herman Rode, as St. Luke in 1484, the gospel he is writing. The Virgin stands in front of him carrying the infant Jesus. Her left index finger points to the book open on a writing stand and next to it is a standing winged ox with a halo; its front paws are astride a paper roll

where the Saint's name is written. It is an angel who guides the hand of Jan Gossaert, as St. Luke in 1525, kneeling before a lectern, painting the Virgin and Child. The Virgin is playing with the Child, whom Dirk Bouts as St. Luke, in 1455, is painting. In 1487 Rueland Frueauf as St. Luke is painting a Virgin who clasps the Child to her; his halo is a cross of light. And is Roger van der Weyden the St. Luke drawing the Virgin with a breast bared, suckling the infant Jesus?

Bornemann, kneeling, appeals for prayers for himself as St. Luke, to whom the altar and altarpiece are dedicated. St. Luke is an intercessor.

Mignard, behind the Saint, holds a scaled-down copy of the portrait St. Luke is finishing. St. Luke is a model.

Ensor, kneeling, a palette in his hand, is St. Luke, seeks to be St. Luke. No end yet to prayer.

Giambattista Tiepolo: *Apelles painting Campaspe before Alexander the Great, 1736-1737, with self-portrait as Apelles*

The Virgin, the courtesan and the painter
or
Eros frigid

Apelles and St. Luke were painters of whose work no token remains.

Venus squeezes and wrings out her wet hair. What is this Aphrodite, this Aphrodite Anadyomene? For us it is nothing; a text is the sole trace of it. Apelles painted her. Similarly he painted the portrait of Alexander's mistress Campaspe. During the sittings Apelles could neither hide nor keep silent about his desire; and Alexander parted with Campaspe and left her with the painter.

The Virgin Mary poses for the painter evangelist. The painter paints. The Virgin poses. The courtesan poses.

In one case, the woman desired; in the other, the woman beyond desire. It is upon these *models*, both irreducible and irreconcilable, that painting is based.

It is the only possible and yet absurd synthesis between praying and desiring, inventing itself as frigid Eros. Painting creates itself as wounded and unsatisfied desire.

"You would take the bottles by the neck, if you were thirsty; the peaches and the grapes whet the appetite and make you want to reach out for them."[1] And the thirst is not quenched; and the hand remains empty.

"This is the right way of approaching or being initiated into the mysteries of love, to begin with examples of beauty in this world, and using them as steps to ascend continually with that absolute beauty as one's aim, from one instance of physical beauty to two and from two to all, then from physical beauty to moral beauty, and from moral beauty to the beauty of knowledge, until from knowledge of various kinds one arrives at the supreme knowledge whose sole object is that absolute beauty, and knows at last what absolute beauty is."[2] Such is the initiation described to Socrates by Diotima. From Campaspe to the Virgin, is it the same initiation? Yes, because here Love is always at work. Love is a great spirit, whose function is: "To interpret and convey messages to the gods from men and to men from the gods, prayers and sacrifices from the one, and commands and rewards from the other. Being of an intermediate nature, Love bridges the gap between them."[3] Love then is the spirit that acts as intermediary between gods and men.

Artemisia Gentileschi:
Self-Portrait as La Pittura, 1638?

La Pittura

"Painting is represented here by a beautiful young woman with black, curly hair, her mouth covered by a bandeau, and a golden chain round her neck with a mask dangling from it. In one hand she has several paint-brushes bearing the motto 'Imitatio' and in the other a picture. She wears a dress of variegated colours. Painting, one of the noblest professions invented by the human mind, is represented as a beautiful woman. This shows that painting is comely and fair and that its beauties charm the human heart. The young woman has thick, curly black hair, because skilled painters, always intent on imitating Nature and Art, and so continually pensive and dreamy, for that reason lapse into a melancholy known to doctors as adust, whose peculiar effect is to produce the kind of hair we have just described.

"Her gagged mouth means that painters generally like to work in silence and solitude, so that their imagination will be all the more lively and forceful. The mask hanging from her neck on a chain signifies that Imitation and Painting are inseparable, and the links of the chain point to the close connection between the two. For it is indeed true, as Cicero states in his treatise on Rhetoric, that the painter does not learn everything from a better master than himself, but that from a single element he gets his ideas which, through their resemblance and similarity, are linked together like a chain. We may add that through the quality of the gold employed in it, one may see that painting is debased for ordinary purposes, unless it is sustained by the generosity of the great. And through the mask one sees that Imitation is perfectly proper for painting.

"As for her dress of variegated colours, it symbolizes the numerous adornments that seem to charm the eye of those who behold them. And the fact that she has covered her feet indicates that proportion, the foundation of this fine art, is something the painter sees in his mind before he paints it in colour: it must remain as if hidden and only see the light of day when the picture is completely finished. In the profession of painting it is a precious secret to possess the gift of painting in such a way that the fairest qualities are only apparent to those with the keenest knowledge."[1]

Artemisia, turning away, is painting. The brush in her right hand moves forward with her raised arm towards an invisible canvas. Her movement is frozen. The upper part of her body leans towards the left. Her gaze seems not to be following the direction of the brush but to be focused on something beyond the painted canvas. The raised right arm, the face and the swell of her breasts revealed by her décolleté are in the light, but her hand, further away, is in the shadow. What certainties is her eye looking for? Artemisia is painting. The model and the canvas are out of sight. Only the gesture of painting is shown.

Her hair is black, dressed in a chignon, and some locks and curls have worked loose. Round her neck there is a long golden chain hanging down over her breast, with a small mask dangling from it.

The written word "Imitation" is nowhere to be seen. The tension of the gaze turned on the model and the gesture of the right hand holding the brush, suspended in mid-air in front of the canvas, are a metaphor of the word. Artemisia's mouth is not gagged. It is because this gag alone is missing that the portrait of the painter does not correspond to La Pittura as described by Ripa. By her dress, by her chain with its dangling mask, by the brushes she holds and her attitude, a metaphor of Imitatio, it is Painting that is portrayed.

Artemisia is not only a painter; she seeks to be, proclaims herself to be, Painting itself. Is this a challenge? Is it humility?

Bourgeois among bourgeois

I work for myself.[1]
Frans Hals

Gathered together on and beside a flight of outdoor steps, the officers and men of the St. George Militia of Haarlem are posing.

On the far right with a standard on his shoulder and a blue sash at his waist is Pieter Schout, whose left fist rests on his hip behind the pommel of his sword. Next to him, a little to the rear, also carrying a standard and bare-headed, is Dirck Dicx. Both Dirck Dicx and Pieter Schout are bachelors; if they weren't, they would not be carrying standards... Then, with his right hand extended over his chest, comes Captain Quirijn Jansz. Damast, a weaver. Behind him, holding a halberd, stands Sergeant Lucas van Tetrode. Opposite Captain Quirijn Jansz. is Captain Nicolaes Grauwert; both are carrying lances. Then, almost in profile, Florens van der Hoef. Behind, practically full face, we see Lieutenant Cornelis Coning who was to be the Burgomaster of Haarlem in 1659 and 1660. Dressed in light-coloured clothes amidst this sombre troop, his hat decorated with a blue feather, is the treasurer Michiel de Wael standing in front of

Lieutenant François Wouters. Finally, on the left is a group of three men: his hands clasped over the pommel of a cane, Colonel Johan Claesz. Loo, Burgomaster of Haarlem, appears to be listening to Lambert Wouters who, on his left, bears an orange standard unfurled on his shoulder; behind them is Sergeant Gabriel Loreyn.

Behind this front row, the remainder of the troop is lined up on the steps. In the middle stands Lieutenant Hendrick Coning; then Sergeant Abraham van der Schalke, an artist and sacristan. Moving to the higher steps we encounter Nicolaes Jansz. van Loo, a sergeant, Hendrick Gerritsz. Pot, lieutenant, and Jacob Druyvesteyn, the shaft of a blue standard on his shoulder. Lastly, at the top of the steps is Sergeant Pieter de Jong and in front of him, almost hidden by the standard and the blade of a halberd, Frans Hals.

In 1618 Frans Hals, like his brother Dirk, was a member of the Arquebusiers of St. George. These are the militiamen he painted in 1639, gathered together in full dress. Three years earlier a decree was enacted obliging such civic guards to reduce the festivities of their annual banquets from one week to four days. These guards were incorporated into the Dutch militia during the eighty years of war against Spain (1568-1648). The civic guards had been created in the fourteenth century, but during Hals's time they only engaged in target practice, and once a year, in the spring, practised shooting popinjays. The targets were placed at the top of a vertical pole. The winner of the competition wore a silver chain for a year as a distinguishing mark. Perhaps this troop is going off to practise?

These men posing are the bourgeois of the city. Burgomasters, aldermen, guild members. They are professors, weavers, tradesmen, merchants, pastors, industrialists. As a group and individually, they have their pictures painted. Their portraits confirm their functions. The portrait is a form of bourgeois enthronement, and the painter who officiates is no different from them. He himself is a bourgeois, a member of a professional guild. Frans Hals among the officers and sergeants of St. George is a bourgeois among bourgeois. In Haarlem being a painter was no different from being a merchant.

◁ Frans Hals:

Self-Portrait (from Officers and Men of the St. George Militia), 1639

Officers and Men of the St. George Militia, 1639

Simon Vouet: *Self-Portrait, 1614-1627?*

Concerning a lock of hair

Over the white collar of Simon Vouet falls a lock of hair longer than the rest. This portrait is from the first quarter of the seventeenth century, and at that time wearing such a lock of hair was a sign of rare elegance. Known in France as *la moustache* or *la cadenette* (long love-lock),[1] this stray lock of hair falls over the shoulder, is left longer than the rest of the hair and sometimes is plaited with a coloured ribbon.

This *moustache* or long love-lock emphasizes the elegance of these fashionable artists. The type of doublet worn here by Vouet was known as a *pourpoint à la grande chiquetade*. In other portraits of the period the long, straggling lock of hair falls over a ruff.

Through the portraits they painted of themselves, painters were making it clear that they claimed a certain social standing, that they didn't belong to just any circles. And it was by this French style of fashion that they distinguished themselves as Frenchmen, even if they happened to be living in Rome.

Portrait of Le Nain by Le Nain

On the 8th of April 1777 a canvas was sold in Paris representing "an artist in his studio painting a portrait." Two years passed and on the 15th of March 1779 the "portrait of Le Nain painted by himself" was sold. The anonymous artist has become Le Nain. On the 14th of April 1784 this portrait was in the salerooms again: "This work, of so fine a colouring and so lifelike, adds to these two qualities the merit of showing us the portrait of this famous painter."

This picture is the portrait of Le Nain by Le Nain. But which of the Le Nains is it? Antoine? Louis? Matthieu?

The painter is seated on a studded red leather chair. "To paint gracefully and with ease, you must hold your brush so that it is as long as possible and you should be sitting upright on your chair (but with no strain) and at a reasonable distance from your work. In this way, what you paint can be handled more freely. Otherwise, nothing takes away from this grace and ease so much as sticking your nose against your canvas (to use the vulgar expression) and holding your brush short." This advice comes from Chapter 29 of *Les premiers éléments de la peinture pratique* (Paris, 1684), a chapter headed: "On grace and ease in painting at the easel." With his right hand held against the handrest, Le Nain is putting a dab of paint on a small canvas. Is he only roughing out his canvas? Is it almost finished? The invisible canvas, its only presence being its thickness, will never permit us to determine what the painter is painting, what portrait, what subject. All one can see is the white thickness folded over the stretcher, the edge of the canvas and the edge of the easel, with neither perspective nor shadow. The painter is painting; what he is painting remains hidden. Probably he is doing the portrait of the man sitting almost opposite him,

Antoine Le Nain: *The Studio, 1645?*

a little to the left of the easel. The left hand resting on the crossed legs holds a hat; the right hand, gloved like the other, lies on the fabric and folds of the coat. The stillness of the hands and the staring eyes, focused it would seem on one of the uprights of the easel or the painter's shoulder, imply the immobility of a pose taken and held. Now the painter is looking neither at his model nor his canvas. He looks away towards a mirror where we are. (It may be that it is not this man seated facing him that he is portraying. What he is painting is quite different, namely someone who is posing in the place where we are.) The painter is posing, watching himself, painting himself.

Two other men are looking at this mirror, the man standing behind the painter and the man standing behind the sitter. These eyes sweep the canvas from right and left. These looks are similar to those of the artist painting his own portrait but can not of themselves class the men as painters. A step back from the chair where the sitter is posing, another man stands in front of the easel, his outspread hand held against his chest. To whom is this gesture addressed, this attitude? What does it mean? Admiration perhaps, affectation? He is draped in a red cloak, a flap-end of which tapers down to a point, fitting neatly into the triangle formed by the uprights of the easel. He holds a palette and this palette designates him as a painter. This man is Le Nain. Antoine? Louis? Matthieu? He is looking towards the painter seated at the easel. Louis? Antoine? Matthieu? Only these two men are quite definitely painters. The standing one holding a palette is looking towards the other, who is looking at the mirror with the gaze of a painter painting himself. Two other men are looking in the same direction as the painter, towards the mirror but there is nothing that labels them as painters. One or the other is Le Nain. Matthieu? Antoine? Louis? Who is it painting? No reply is possible. Shortly, the man who sitting down dabs a touch of paint on the canvas, will rise and leave his place to the other man standing near the model, a palette ready in his hand.

An artist in his studio is "painting a portrait." The studio is neither described nor shown. The shadowy obscure background is neither a setting nor a place. In the same way that we can't say with certainty who is who, we can't say where we are. Neither identity nor place is stated. The place is neutral and matters little, just as it matters little to know who is the man painting there. Antoine? Louis? Matthieu? A painter is painting and we don't need to know more. Painting is the only issue. An easel, brushes, palettes, a hand-rest, a sitter, a finished portrait on the floor leaning against the chair where the model sits, everything points to the act of painting and this act alone. This portrait of the painter by himself in the act of painting is an understatement. Le Nain is painting. The man painting is named Le Nain.

The canvas is neither signed nor dated. The model posing gives us the date. The cut of his moustache, his boots, his breeches tell us the period: about 1645.

On the first of December 1646 Louis, Antoine and Matthieu Le Nain made over their assets reciprocally to each other.

"The undersigned honourable persons appeared before the notaries at the Châtelet, Paris: Antoine, Louis and Matthieu Le Nain, painters at Paris, residing together at the Faubourg St. Germain, rue du Vieil Colombier, in the Parish of St. Sulpice, who considering the length of time they have dwelt there and have worked together without being separated, and the efforts each of them has made individually to acquire and preserve the few assets it has pleased God to dispense to them, and given the love and affection they bear each other, and further pertinent considerations inspiring them hereto, have, by these presents, and in due and proper form, made a gift *inter vivos* of all their goods and chattels and property both moveable and immoveable that may at the present time belong to any one of them, and that on the day of the death of any one of them shall likewise belong to them for their enjoyment as follows: on the death of the first of the three, these properties shall be divided into equal parts between the two survivors, their heirs and assigns jointly and severally, this being agreed upon by the aforesaid survivors, and after the death of one of the two aforesaid survivors, the whole shall then belong to the last surviving of the aforesaid heirs and assigns in unrestricted ownership and without any encumbrances, always provided that at the time of the death of the aforesaid persons (being the first deceased) there are no children born in lawful wedlock, in which case, the present deed shall become operative in respect of the aforesaid children of the aforementioned initially deceased persons and the survivor; and thence by direct descent to the surviving children and to their children. This present deed is set down in authentic form and by virtue of the fraternal good friendship they all feel for one another and with the aim of mutually rewarding each other. And in order to register these presents at the record office of registrations of the aforesaid Châtelet, and at all other places where it may be required, they have named and established as their procurator the bearer of these presents and have given him power of attorney to obtain any requisite documents, because thus, etc., each acting in his own right, etc. Done and executed in the chambers of Hervy, one of the undersigned notaries, in the year 1646, on the first day of December, at ten o'clock of the morning, drawn up and sealed by the aforesaid Hervy. Signed d'Orléans and Hervy, and subsequently submitted for registration as follows: In the year 1646, on Tuesday the 4th of December, the present contract of mutual deed was taken to the record office of the Châtelet, Paris, and there registered."[1]

One phrase here is of more interest to us than all the rest: "Who considering the length of time they have dwelt there and have worked together without being separated..."

Le Nain is the name of the man painting at the easel, but which of the three brothers he may be, there is no way of knowing. This portrait of Le Nain by Le Nain is their common will and testament.

Judith and Holofernes, David and Goliath
(questions)

The severed head of Holofernes that Judith is carrying, her fist clasping the hair, is wrinkled and already has the pallor of death. Cristofano Allori portrays himself as Holofernes and his mistress was the model who posed for Judith. Was this grim scene meant to symbolize some form of love-death?

Could it be Cranach himself who is this Holofernes, his eyelids still open in death, a severed head that Judith, gloved and smiling, holds on to by the hairs at the temple?

Could Simon Vouet be this young man with the bare shoulder, the David carrying the severed head of Goliath, the dead Philistine? David the shepherd, the king and the lover of the Song of Songs?

Similarly, could Poussin be David?

So many questions. Is the painter Holofernes *castrated* or the murderous lover whose name is "as ointment poured forth?"[1] The answers are also questions.

1. Attributed to Poussin: *David with the Head of Goliath, early or mid-17th century*
2. Cristofano Allori: *Judith with the Head of Holofernes, early 17th century*
3. Lucas Cranach the Elder: *Self-Portrait, c. 1530*
4. Lucas Cranach the Elder: *Judith with the Head of Holofernes, 1530*
5. Simon Vouet: *Self-Portrait, early 17th century*
6. Simon Vouet: *David, early 17th century*
7. Artemisia Gentileschi: *Judith with the Head of Holofernes, early 17th century*
8. Artemisia Gentileschi: *Self-Portrait as La Pittura, 1638?*

Could Artemisia Gentileschi be this Judith turning towards the camp of the assassinated general that she has just left with her servant who is carrying the head in a basket? Could Artemisia Gentileschi be this Judith who looks back at Bethulia, the crime now committed, and whose only troubled thought is that of flight?

Reserve and severity

*My nature forces me to seek out
and love well-ordered things; to fly
from confusion which is as adverse
and inimical to me as darkness is
to light.*[1]

Poussin

Poussin's letters tell a definite story about his portraits. From Rome on the 7th of April 1647, he writes to his friend Chantelou in Paris: "There is now nobody in Rome who does a good portrait, which is why I won't be sending you the one you want so soon." Chantelou has not yet been able to persuade Poussin to paint his own portrait; the months pass.

To Chantelou, from Rome, the 22nd of December 1647: "As for my portrait, I'll do my best to give you satisfaction."

Who will paint the portrait? Nothing is yet decided. To Chantelou, from Rome, the 2nd of August 1648: "I would already have had my portrait done to send to you as you wish. But it angers me to spend about ten pistoles for a head in the style of Mignard who is the person I know who does the best ones, although they are cold, finicking, glossed over, and lacking any facility or force." Nearly another year goes by before a decision is taken. From Rome, the 24th of May 1649: "And about my portrait, I shall not fail either to send it to you immediately it is done." On the 20th of June 1649: "I've done one of my portraits and I shall soon start the other. I'll send the better of the two, but please say nothing about it, so as not to cause any jealousy." On the 8th of October 1649: "I'll do my best to send you my portrait at the end of this year." The months go by. On the 22nd of January 1650: "I would by now have kept the promise I made you to send you my portrait, if my desire to do so had not met with an obstacle. I beg of you to believe that it particularly displeases me to make you wait so long, and that as soon as I find it possible, I shall keep my promise." On the 13th of March 1650: "It would be with great pleasure that I would answer your last letter if I had some good news for you about the pictures I promised you, but particularly about my portrait that I haven't yet been able to finish. I confess naïvely that I'm lazy in doing this work, in which I take no pleasure and am little accustomed to, because it is twenty-eight years since I've painted a portrait. Nonetheless I must finish, because I far prefer your satisfaction to my own." Finally, on the 29th of May 1650: "I have finished the portrait you want of me. I could send it to you by the next regular mail. But the badgering of some of my friends who want a copy of it will cause some delay.

Nonetheless I'll send it to you as soon as possible. Monsieur Pointel shall have the one I promised him at the same time, and I trust you won't be jealous of this, because I've kept the promise I made you and have chosen the better picture and better likeness for you: you'll see the difference yourself. I maintain that you should see in this portrait a token of the willingness to serve that I have pledged to you, all the more because I wouldn't do what I have done for you in this matter for anyone else alive. I wouldn't care to tell you what trouble I've had in doing this portrait, for fear you might think that I wish to show it off. It will be enough when I hear that it has pleased you." The portrait is in Chantelou's possession. On the 3rd of July 1650 Poussin writes to him a last time about this portrait which might need to be varnished on its arrival in Paris. (Writing about a canvas Chantelou had received four years earlier, Poussin said: "If by any chance you find some mould on this one, don't be at all surprised, because it's only varnished with egg-white, which you can remove with water and a sponge, and afterwards have it varnished with a thin, light varnish.")[2] "The prominence you want to give my portrait in your house greatly increases my debt to you. It will hang there as worthily as did the picture of Virgil in the museum of Augustus. I shall be just as proud of it as if it were in the collection of the dukes of Tuscany with the Leonardos, Michelangelos and Raphaels."

Chantelou looks at Poussin's portrait. He reads the Latin inscription painted in behind the painter, at shoulder height on the right of the canvas, darkened by the shadow of the head: "Effigies Nicolai Poussini Andelyensis Pictoris. Anno Ætatis. 56. Romae Anno Iubilei 1650." Nicolas Poussin says he comes from Les Andelys, and his self-portrait is dated in Rome; nothing else. No title. Poussin is a member of the St. Luke Academy in Rome; Poussin is the premier painter in ordinary to the King of France; nothing is said of this. Vertically below this inscription is the painter's right hand, with a ring on the little finger, resting on a portfolio tied with a knotted red ribbon. Possibly Chantelou is aware that the stone of this ring has the following words engraved on it: "Confiance de Nicolas Poussin." Is the painter standing or sitting? Probably sitting. Most likely the portfolio is in his lap. The painter's left hand is perhaps resting on his knee if we judge by the angle of the black cloak on the left arm. The

Nicolas Poussin: *Self-Portrait, 1650*

patch of ornamented red, most likely close-woven velvet, behind the painter, is the back of a chair or an armchair. On the floor, leaning against the wall, are framed canvases; these frames are of the same type that Poussin recommends Chantelou to use: "When you have received your picture I beg of you, if you like it, to decorate it with a piece of cornice, because it needs it, so that if you consider all the different parts of the canvas, the line of sight should be held in focus and not spread out beyond the picture and allowed to take in the shapes of other nearby objects, which would then enter pell-mell into the painted ones and create confusion. It would be most suitable just to put matt gold on this cornice, because it blends very softly with the colours and doesn't clash with them."[3] The picture behind the painter is still blank, the last one against the wall with a wider frame is reversed. Between these two canvases are two more; only a section of the frame of one of them shows it is there. Of the other, you can only see the blue strip of a sky and the face and bust of a crowned woman, with two male arms reaching out for her shoulders. This canvas present behind the painter is not a passage repeated from an earlier picture. This would appear to be the only intimation of it that we have. Why is it there and what does it stand for? The diadem the woman is wearing is a sort of mask with open eyes. Does she represent Painting? And the outstretched arms and the smile: could they signify Friendship? Or is this woman the Hera of the *Iliad*, the "ox-eyed Hera" whom Zeus is reaching out to embrace? Like Bellori in 1672, like Lorenzo Bernini in 1664, Chantelou no doubt saw this as a reassurance of friendship, a reassurance like that of the painter's letters, concealed here by a chair-back and a canvas, an understatement as the canvases and the portfolio are an understatement of painting. The other portrait of Poussin by himself, which he sent to Pointel, lacks this severe restraint. The inscription on it ("NICOLAUS POUSSINUS ANDELYENSIS ACADEMICUS ROMANUS PRIMUS PICTOR ORDINARIUS LUDOVICI JUSTI REGIS GALLIAE. ANNO DOMINI 1649. ROMAE. ÆTATIS SUAE 55") in which he describes himself as an academician in Rome and the premier painter of the King of France, together with the book he holds – no ring now on the finger of the hand – with the title on the spine ("DE LUMINE ET COLORE") and the pencil in his left hand (an avowal of the mirror), all reassert that Poussin is a painter and a painter with titles to his name.

The portrait chosen by Chantelou was chosen by him because it was the "better likeness." This likeness is not only a question of the facial features; its likeness to the man lies also in its restraint, reserve and severity.

The key and the cross

A portrait of a man. Where? Nowhere. The background lost in shadow is not a place. Unspecified, it is only an absence. A man is posing. Standing, with his right hand ungloved at an angle resting on his hip; his elbow is bent and he turns away slightly. He is clothed in black. The head is set on a fine, white, oblique collar like a tray or a disk, like a sharp bright blade between the neck and the hair. The dark hair is apparently separated by a middle parting from which, thick and straight, it divides to frame the face (the beard seems to be added). The head is three-quarters turned towards the viewer, the torso less so. The pommel and hilt of a sword can be seen against the hollow of the left elbow above a glove, leather perhaps, of which the fold covers part of the arm. The belt buckle is indistinct and only sketchily indicated. To the right, held by the belt, and well in evidence, is a key; its barrel is hidden by the folds of the sleeve at the point where the elbow bends. No text, no inscription: neither the name nor the age nor the occupation of this model are given. Silence. This portrait is a man's portrait. At the court of Philip IV of Spain – this man is wearing the austere black clothes the King insisted on – those chosen by the King as *ayuda de cámara* (valet de chambre) wore a black key at the waist. The golden key such as the Count-Duke of Olivares carried was the emblem worn only by the gentlemen of the chamber. This black key was an honour to which many knights of the military Orders aspired. There were no gentlemen ushers at the Madrid Court. Thus it was important to be one of the King's *valets de chambre*. This male portrait from the Uffizi Gallery is the portrait of a *valet de chambre* of Philip IV, King of Spain. This *valet de chambre* of the King is Diego Velázquez.

In 1656 we find Velázquez painting *Las Meninas*. The painter's studio is one of the rooms of what were formerly the apartments in the Alcázar of Prince Baltasar Carlos, who had died ten years earlier in 1646; he had been betrothed to Mariana of Austria, the current Queen. The Infanta Margarita and her entourage have entered a few minutes earlier and their appearance will have interrupted the painter's work to welcome them as etiquette dictates. Then Velázquez turns back to his canvas, wielding his brushes now in the silence of the rustling dresses and the low murmur of voices. But this visit is no doubt unexpected and it is not governed by etiquette. The dog, a Castilian mastiff, lies on the floor at the feet of the two dwarfs who have accompanied the Empress: Mari-Bárbola in a grey dress and Nicolasito Pertusato putting his left foot on the dog's haunch. Behind them the rest of the group has halted a short distance behind the canvas, immobile. Doña Isabel de Velasco, her

Diego Velázquez: *Self-Portrait, c. 1631*

white hands encircled by black lace with a red bow, and resting on the crinoline of her grey dress, leans slightly forward towards the Infanta to whom Doña María Augustina de Sarmiento, kneeling in front of the canvas almost in profile, proffers with her right hand a silver tray bearing a red pitcher and some wafers or perhaps biscuits. Standing back in the shadows behind Doña Isabel de Velasco we see Doña Marcela de Ulloa – in charge of serving the Queen's ladies-in-waiting – and, perhaps, Don Ruiz de Azcona. In the background, on the stairs leading to the open door, Don José Nieto Veláz-

Diego Velázquez: *Self-Portrait, 1656 (from Las Meninas)*

set up on the left, reinforced by the slats of the stretchers and held by an easel, a diagonal section of which is visible.

I look at the canvas: the painter, the Infanta, her suite, her duennas and her dwarfs are looking at me. Occupying the King's place, I am a usurper. This canvas is for the King's eyes, for his eyes only. Velázquez is painting the King. Velázquez is painting for the King. He is standing in front of the picture. His left arm partially bent, he holds his palette laid out with colours. His thumb in the palette hole appears as a lighter patch above the brushes bunched together. The brush in the right hand, held somewhat higher, points towards the palette. Above the palette and the paint-brush, showing red against his black-clothed chest, there is a cross, the Cross of the Knights of the Order of Santiago. The cross and the palette are incompatible. For a long time the grandees of Spain refused to allow the painter Velázquez to be ennobled by the King. It was not sufficient to have the 148 attestations to his "*nobleza limpieza*"; nor the King's favour for the "*aposentador de Palacio*" (Grand Marshal of the Palace), a position to which he was appointed on the 16th of February 1652 solely due to the King's efforts (he took the oath on the 8th of March of the same year), having been elevated to this rank despite the unfavourable opinions of five members of a special commission – for Velázquez was a painter! No, the Pope had to intervene. In 1650 the Holy See informed the Apostolic Nuncio in Madrid that His Holiness supported the request made by Velázquez to be awarded the Spanish Military Order.

More than thirty years after Velázquez had been appointed Court Painter on the 6th of October 1623, the King at last made him a Knight of the Order of Santiago; the date was the 28th of November 1659.

Being a painter merits no consideration of any kind. A painter who seeks to become a knight is guilty of impertinence . . . In the eighteenth century the following story was still being told in Madrid. A certain Jesus of Nazareth requested admission to the Order of St. James. He was rejected. Such an honour could not be extended to the son of Joseph, a carpenter, and Mary, a dressmaker.[1] Velázquez was only a courtier; his sole importance lay in his being the King's confidant. "How could you make a mistake like that with a man so appreciated by the King, one who talks for hours together with His Majesty?"[2] asked an irritated grandee of Spain whose son had dared to speak a few irate words to Velázquez.

The mirror is an understatement. The King is absent; his absence is an affirmation of the need for his presence. The palette, the brush, and the cross, in such proximity, are a scandal that the King alone accepts. Such proximity is inconceivable at the Court of Spain and must be invisible. So one must of necessity occupy the King's place to see it and to accept it.

The key: Velázquez is a *valet de chambre* of the King. The cross: Velázquez is knighted by the King.

He paints for the King alone.

quez, Marshal of the Palace, is either leaving or entering. In this room lit only by daylight, for no chandelier hangs from the two sombre ornate ceiling hooks visible . . . in this room with its white walls hung with pictures, such as *Pallas and Arachne* copied from Rubens and *Apollo and Marsyas* copied from Jordaens, and others too, suspended between the window recesses, although the perspective is such that only the thick black frames are visible, Velázquez is painting. Behind him, hanging between two doors beneath the copies of Rubens and Jordaens there is a mirror and its lacklustre gleam reveals the reflection of Philip IV and Queen Mariana.

This mirror, disregarded by all, fails to tell the truth. It remains silent about this visit to this room in the Alcázar Palace. It pays no attention to the Infanta, her suite or the painter. This scorned mirror shows what the Infanta, her entourage and the painter himself are looking at, namely King Philip IV and Queen Mariana who, standing quite still in front of a red curtain held in place by a loop, are posing. Velázquez is painting the portrait of the King and the Queen, and for us this portrait is no more than the unseen reverse side of the tall canvas

Diego Velázquez: *Las Meninas or The Maids of Honour, 1656*

Jean-Baptiste de Champaigne and Nicolas de Platte-Montagne:
Double Portrait of the Two Artists, 1654

Wilhelm von Schadow: *Triple Portrait of the Artist,*
his Brother Rudolf, and Bertel Thorvaldsen, 1814

Friendship

This is a double portrait. Nicolas de Platte-Montagne is holding out his open right hand towards Jean-Baptiste de Champaigne, seated facing him. Between them, on the back of an unrolled drawing, the period, with the written date 1654. Nicolas de Platte-Montagne and Jean-Baptiste de Champaigne have similar movements of the head and torso as they turn towards someone looking at them, some third person who has interrupted them and to whom they are introducing themselves. Jean-Baptiste was drawing; Nicolas was playing the cello or was about to; he still holds a hat in his right hand. They are in a studio. Books, sketches, brushes and a palette are scattered about the table; another palette is hanging on the wall under a shelf containing a statuette, a flask, and a bust that may be of Seneca. These two young men who have been interrupted turn round, smile and introduce themselves.

On the board that Jean-Baptiste de Champaigne holds at an angle on the table are the words: *N. Montaigne pinxit me.* Was it to bring the name into line with that of his friend Champaigne that the spelling Montaigne was used?

On the easel standing behind Nicolas de Platte-Montagne is another inscription: *J. B. de Champaigne me fecit.*

N. Montaigne pinxit me, J. B. de Champaigne me fecit: N. M. painted me, J. B. de C. made me. These two answering statements consummate the exchange.

Nicolas de Platte-Montagne doesn't sign the portrait he painted of Jean-Baptiste de Champaigne, but says that the latter is the maker of his own. And reciprocally. The signatures countersign; they vouch for a mutual solidarity.

This double portrait is the portrait of a friendship, a token of exchange and solidarity.

Another studio. In Rome. The window open behind a curtain with rings sliding on a horizontal rod gives on the Colosseum. Three men. Young artists. They are swearing an oath. It is 1814. Doubtless they are familiar with Act One, Scene Two, of Schiller's *Robbers*, in which Karl and his followers are taking an oath in this inn on the Saxon border. An oath of fidelity and obedience. The oaths exchanged bind Karl "*bei dieser männlichen Rechte!*" (twice this virile right hand is invoked). Is it this particular oath, written by Schiller in 1781, that obsesses these three young Germans with their artists' berets? Or was it another? Romanticism was not sparing of oaths. The subject of the oath sworn here by Wilhelm and Rudolf von Schadow and Bertel Thorvaldsen is not death but art. They are holding a mallet, chisels and a palette, and in Rome it is fame they are all challenging beside this marble statue of a young seated girl, tying her sandal. (This

Heinrich Jacob Aldenrath and Friedrich Carl Gröger:
Double Self-Portrait of the Two Artists, 1801

sculpture was to be purchased in 1817 by Prince
Ludwig of Bavaria, heir to the throne.) Through
the Schadow brothers sculpture and painting were
allied, and also through Thorvaldsen, who after his
Triumph of Alexander earned the name of "patriarch
of the bas-relief." Taken all together the various
elements of this oath form a challenge that unites
them: their nationality is apparent in the berets
typical of German artists; the place is shown to be
Rome by the Colosseum visible through the window; and the date on the unfinished sculpture tells
us when they were working.

In 1826 Julius Milde painted the same kind of
challenge, the same kind of oath. He painted himself with Speckter and Oldach.

In the era of Romanticism such oaths implied
complicity and friendship, the latter being tender
and demanding solidarity, both generous and
critical.

The 1801 double portrait of Heinrich Jacob Aldenrath and Friedrich Carl Gröger with his hand
on his friend's shoulder seated at the foot of a tree is
such a portrait of friendship. In 1784 in Edinburgh
John Brown painted himself with Alexander
Runciman. In August of that year 1784 John
Brown wrote to the Earl of Buchan: "Yesterday I
was with Runciman and I sat for the portrait that
he's doing of me on the same canvas where he has
already painted himself. This work is to go to your
Lordship and I think it will be an admirable work.
He has depicted himself seated at his work, palette
and brushes in one hand and a pencil case in the
other. I myself, behind him, examining his work..."

In one case we see the strict demands of friendship; in the other, the tenderness it offers.

In 1805 Philipp Otto Runge painted his own
portrait with his wife and his brother. Fingers ent-
wined, a hand on a shoulder, another held to a
brow, heads bent to one side: *We Three*, the picture
is called. Destroyed by fire in 1931 (a copy of it by
Julius von Ehren survives), this canvas was the very
model and definition of tender romantic friendship.
As at the end of the century Vincent van Gogh was
only able to live and paint thanks to the money his
brother Theo sent him month after month, so
Philipp Otto Runge lived only on what his brother
gave him.

Such pictures were an expression of friendship
and trust, secret in their full implications, public in
their explicit affirmation of mutual confidence and
understanding.

Philipp Otto Runge:
*We Three (The Artist with his Wife Pauline
and his Brother Daniel), 1805*

Morituri . . .

Nearly innocent of all skin and flesh, the skulls of
Hans Burgkmair and his wife appear in the mirror;
she is smiling and he sketches a gesture of resigna-
tion. This was in 1529.

In 1888 a full-length skeleton, its skull covered
with dishevelled and stiffened hair, is said by James
Ensor to be his portrait in 1960.

From century to century, the painter paints the
constant threat that is death. To paint oneself,
reiterated evidence, is to paint a person who will
die. The skull is death itself; the skull is a pretext for
meditating on the only certainty that life is
prepared to enunciate: death.

What a lot of studios there are where among the
plaster casts, the accessories required for painting
such as palettes, brushes and easels, there is a skull
lying about somewhere, on a table or a shelf; it is a
sort of posthumous portrait. Death reminders not-
withstanding, the painters go on painting. Johann
Zoffany in the eighteenth century has in his right
hand one of these grinning skulls and in his left
holds out an hour-glass; time, imperturbable sand,
flows there. Behind this hour-glass, on the cover of
a closed book, is this inscription in roman capitals:

ARS LONGA. VITA BREVIS

Art is long, life is short. And Zoffany is laughing. A
young man wearing a three-cornered hat, seated
behind his easel from which a violin hangs, Gerrit
Bakhuizen is smiling. Over his shoulder, a skull.

1. Hans Burgkmair: *Self-Portrait with his Wife,*
   copy by Lucas Furtenagel from the lost original of 1529

2. Johann Zoffany: *Self-Portrait, 1776*

3. Gerrit Bakhuizen: *Self-Portrait, early 18th century*

4. Filippo Balbi: *Self-Portrait, 1873*

5. Arnold Böcklin: *Self-Portrait with Death playing*
   the Fiddle, 1872

Behind Filippo Balbi, standing, with his foot on a chair, as he starts a drawing in an open sketchbook which he holds on his knee, a skull lies on the table. He clasps a sheet of paper on which is written:

Non è la Sapienza e il merito
che governano la vita, ma la Fortuna
La Fortuna è donna, volubile, capricciosa,
come tutte quelle del suo Sesso.

"It isn't Wisdom and Merit that govern life, but Fortune. Fortune is a woman, fickle, capricious, like all her sex." It is in death (the skull reminds us) that this life will end, a life governed only by fortune. And despite this macabre uncertainty and this proclamation of disillusioned misogynous distrust, the painter is beginning a drawing.

Arnold Böcklin pauses. In his left hand he holds a palette stained with colour, and in his right, his fingers closing on a brush seem to be suspended in motion. Probably he was about to put a different colour on the brush when . . . He turns away, tense and serious, and listens. Death, behind him, grinning, is playing a single-stringed fiddle. The emaciated hand, a skeleton with lacklustre skin stretched over it, grips the bow. What pulsating music is Death playing?

Lovis Corinth: *Self-Portrait with Skeleton, 1896*

Before the glass window of a studio looking out on the roofs of a city, Lovis Corinth stands next to a skeleton, hanging on a vertical rod, curved at the top and ending in a hook. The anatomy skeleton is hanging upright near the painter who wears a check shirt. His hair is short, his moustache full, his chin thick and heavy. In a few years' time . . .

The self-portrait is a meditation. Like the repentant Magdalen staring at the empty eye sockets of a skull, the painter is pensive. "Did these bones cost no more the breeding, but to play at loggats with 'em? Mine ache to think on't."[1]

Vanity, vanity, all is vanity.

Various objects, symbols of the sciences and the arts, are scattered on a table where there are some flowers beginning to wilt. These flowers are another kind of hour-glass. Time withers. Time creates ruins and wrinkles. It is this serene dispair that is proclaimed by the Vanitas still lifes. On the edge of a table, held by open books, hangs a portrait: that of the painter himself.

Adriaen Valck painted this Vanitas still life in about 1660, some twenty years after Bailly had invented the theme of the self-portrait among the objects of a Vanitas picture, an object among fugitive and futile objects. The variations on this theme were numerous in the Netherlands in the second half of the seventeenth century, just as since the outset of this century variations on Democritus' laugh and Heraclitus' tears around a sphere or a globe were numerous; Jacob de Gheyn in 1603 was the first to put them in a Vanitas picture. Neither the tears of one nor the laughter of the other change anything; what do tears or laughter matter? What remains is impotence and ineluctability.

These portraits of men who were going to die are a paradox. Death threatens them and their portrait is a challenge, a prayer, perhaps a certainty. The portrait denies death; it is memory; it calls upon the viewer to remember. Beyond the belief in an eternal life that skulls imply, another kind of immortality is created: memory.

Adriaen Valck: *Vanitas Still Life with Self-Portrait, c. 1660*

Charles Le Brun: *Self-Portrait, 1684*

The abbot and the grand duke
or
The request and the order

Born you were by happy fortune in
Louis's time.
A painter he required, and you a
patron. [1]
Philippe Quinault

"If instead of all the passions we have just spoken of, joy seizes the soul, the movements that express it are very different from those we have just noticed, because in this passion the brow is unfurrowed, the eyebrow motionless, attracted by the surroundings, the eye half open and laughing, the pupil lively and brilliant, the nostrils imperceptibly open, the mouth will have the corners slightly raised, the complexion will be zestful, the cheeks and lips bright red." [2] (This aspect of a portrait should not be neglected: "Expressions are the touchstone of the painter's spirit. He demonstrates by the rightness of the way in which he shows them, his insight and discernment: but the spectator must possess the same spirit in order correctly to perceive them, as the painter does in order to represent them well. A picture should be regarded as a stage is, where each figure plays its role. Well-drawn and well-coloured figures are in truth admirable.") [3] The portrait of Le Brun, handed over on the 29th of November 1684 to the Abbot Charles Antoine de Gondi, Secretary of State of the Grand Duchy of Tuscany, was ordered by Cosimo III at the beginning of 1683; we have a description of it. The joy which was sought, an understatement, becomes serene assurance. But it is not joy alone to which the portrait of Le Brun confesses. Cosimo III asked Le Brun for his self-portrait. Le Brun replied:

"Monseigneur,

Having contemplated the very humble favours I should render your Most Serene Highness for the present You honour me with, and for the honour You are doing me at the same time in asking me for my portrait, I finally thought it my duty to give You my thanks for that which You desire from me, and for the things Your Highness has sent me, albeit these are of infinite value. Because finally that which Your generous hand gives me is only a token of Your ordinary munificence, but that which Your Highness desires to receive from my hand demonstrates a special kindness that I have never merited, and which gives me self-respect but causes me no vanity. I am indeed convinced that my portrait is not worthy of a place in that famous collection where all the most beautiful things are to be seen. But it is not for me to refuse Your Most Serene Highness, above all when You are asking so little of me without which You would never be content. How could I refuse my portrait, I who would achieve so much glory by giving myself in person to

Your Highness, if the service of the greatest King of the world did not keep me in Paris?"[4]

"How could I refuse my portrait, I who would achieve glory by giving myself in person to His Highness, if the service of the greatest King of the world did not keep me in Paris?" Le Brun proclaims this adherence to the King whose name remains unspecified; the title is enough to announce the name. This adherence is essential: having been said, it must still be painted. On the stone parapet on which the painter is leaning with his elbows, the following inscription is engraved:

C. LE BRUN Pr PEINTRE DU ROY TRES CHRESTIEN

Again the king's name is unstated. The king's presence is not proclaimed by a mere inscription on the stones on which the painter is leaning. Fixed to a ribbon knotted under the lace ruffle hangs an oval miniature mounted in a frame set with diamonds; it is the King's portrait, presented by him to his premier painter in 1667. Le Brun is an adherent of the "greatest King of the world," he is the First Painter of the "most Christian king" whose portrait hangs upon his chest. The omission of the name is the affirmation of something evident. The portrait of the painter is the portrait of the King's painter; it is as much the affirmation of this adherence as it is a portrait. The portrait itself would not exist without this affirmation. Lacking it, it would have no being. On the 20th of November 1684 the portrait was completed. Le Brun wrote to the Grand Duke:

"Monseigneur,

If there is anything which could excuse me for not having more promptly satisfied the wish expressed to me by Your Most Serene Highness, it is the shame of sending him a portrait and copies of my works which hardly deserve the honour of being seen by Your Highness. I hope that Your Highness will have the goodness to pardon me for so well founded a timidity and that You will add this favour to those You have already shown me. I shall keep the memory of them my whole life through and will continue to proclaim them, so as to make known to all the true feelings of gratitude, submission and respect which I have retained for Your Most Serene Highness. I have never derived pleasure from being known by the features of my countenance, but it will be glorious for me to be distinguished by these keen impressions of my zeal, which shall ever be to demonstrate with how much ardour and respect I shall be my whole life, etc."[4]

LE BRUN

"I have never derived pleasure from being known by the features of my countenance." Le Brun's memory has failed him; it is true that thirty years have passed since the 16th of December 1654, the day on which he signed a contract with Monsieur Olier, at the time parish priest of Saint-Sulpice; he was to paint ten canvases for the Seminary. *The Descent of the Holy Ghost* was the first one finished. "Monsieur Le Brun having surpassed himself in this picture, he asked Monsieur Olier's permission to portray himself in it. Which he obtained and in fact portrayed himself as an apostle, but at the edge and looking at the spectators. His reason was that when people cast eyes on the picture, at the same time they should recognize the painter and so convey to its author the esteem and praise his work merited."[5] He was to be paid 900 livres for the work; Monsieur de Bretonvilliers withheld his consent for the additional ten pistoles the painter asked for.

In 1654 Le Brun had to seek permission to portray himself as an apostle in *The Descent of the Holy Ghost*. In 1684 Le Brun painted the portrait of the First Painter of the King at the request of His Most Serene Highness Cosimo III. When the painter wants to paint himself, he can't do so without permission; when his portrait is required of him – a grand duke's request in 1683 was a form of command – it is not at all the portrait of Le Brun that goes on to canvas but the portrait of the First Painter of the King, by the First Painter of the King. By his own request, he portrays himself as an apostle; by order, he paints the portrait of the King's First Painter. His portraits will only have been his masks. Le Brun never did portray himself in the first person singular.

The apostle calls out for glory; the First Painter no longer lays claim to it. To serve the king suffices; this service is his glory.

Charles Le Brun: *The Descent of the Holy Ghost, 1656-1657?*

Posthumous assassination

Great men, Colbert, are poor courtiers,
Little inclined to truckling duties.

Molière

And Molière adds: "Who gives himself to court life is lost to art."[1]

Le Brun was the courtier whom Molière had in mind. But these hard sayings, in neat alexandrines, were powerless in 1669. Colbert was Le Brun's protector and it was difficult to attack him successfully. Louis XIV interrupted the Council so that everyone could be shown the *Raising of the Cross* which he had just received from Le Brun.

"His Majesty ennobled him; honoured him with the Order of St. Michael and made him his First Painter. When the King chose Le Brun as First Painter, at the same time he made him the director of the Gobelins tapestry factory."[2]

Le Brun, the King's First Painter and director of the Gobelins works, was also director, life chancellor and rector of the Royal Academy of Painting and Sculpture.

"I have long been accustomed to preferential treatment. It is this that animates and strengthens men of genius," says he.[3] Mignard is not even an academician and doesn't want to be one. Mignard is waiting. In 1683 Colbert dies. Le Brun, who at this time was completing his Hall of Mirrors decorations at Versailles, is unable to account for the three million livres he had received from the now deceased Comptroller of Finances. Only one million seven hundred thousand livres were spent. There is said to be a warrant of arrest for Le Brun, who risks incarceration in the Bastille. Louis XIV walks into one of the rooms at Versailles, goes up to Le Brun and asks: "Is something the matter, Monsieur Le Brun? You have served me usefully and successfully for too long for me to forget you." Le Brun stays on. Mignard is left waiting.

The Hall of Mirrors is complete, Colbert is dead, royal orders of any importance are becoming increasingly rare, but Le Brun stays on. At Montmorency he falls ill; the King sends him his own doctor.[4] Mignard is waiting and his hate is unchanged. Louvois, protector of the Academy, can do nothing.

Mignard is waiting. Le Brun dies.

Le Brun is dead.

"Today the first of March, one thousand six hundred and ninety, the King being at Versailles and wishing to fill the post of his First Painter left vacant by the decease of Seigneur Le Brun, thought he could make no better choice than in the person of Mignard, by virtue both of His Majesty's knowledge of his great ability, and the universal reputation he has acquired in this art, as well as the great number of fine works that he has done in the Château of Versailles and in the châteaux of royal personages, which are like so many imprints for posterity of his skill and merit, which gives His Majesty to believe that nothing can contribute more to bringing perfection to painting than by placing the examination and direction of the future works to be created for His Majesty in the hands of so excellent a master; which is why His Majesty has kept and is still keeping the aforesaid Sieur Mignard in the position of office of his First Painter, now vacant through the death of the aforesaid Sieur Le Brun. It is the King's wish that Sieur Mignard assume the latter's functions, under the orders of the Superintendent and Director of his Buildings, Arts and Manufactures of France, and that he should enjoy the same honours, authority, prerogatives, preeminences, immunities, liberties, earnings amounting to twelve hundred livres, liveries to the amount of two thousand livres, together with other rights and advantages forming part of the aforesaid position and that to this effect he shall be employed in the quarters of the Officers of the King's Household and Buildings, and be paid his wages and entitlements by the treasurers of the King's Household and Buildings aforementioned, all this to commence on the day of the death of the aforesaid Sieur Le Brun, by virtue of the present royal warrant, that His Majesty in the expression of his will has signed with his own hand."[5]

From then on, Louvois could do anything.

"Monsieur de la Chapelle has told us that the King granted Monsieur Mignard, in consideration of his rare merit and of the excellence of his works, the office of his First Painter, together with all the titles, honours, prerogatives and employments previously enjoyed by the late Monsieur Le Brun. In particular, concerning the Academy, the post of Academician, the office of Rector and the rank of Chancellor and Director of the Company. Monseigneur de Louvois, our Protector, had called upon him to make a declaration of this order to the Academy, his intention being that the order should be executed. Having heard the declaration, the Company spoke with one voice, saying aloud that there was no need to deliberate on such an occasion, nor to tally votes either by beans or some other method, since it was a matter of showing respectful obedience to the King's wishes and submission to the orders of our distinguished Protector, which it will always carry out with great joy, and above all on this occasion when the Company was to receive within its ranks a man of such outstanding merit for whom it had always felt great esteem. All that it wished of him was to see him enjoy for long years the honours he had so well deserved. And for these reasons the Company paid no heed to the ordinary procedures or to what is specified in the statutes, namely a progression from Academician to Assistant Professor, from Assistant Professor to Professor, from Professor to Assistant Rector, and from Assistant Rector to Rector.

"Thus it resolved to dispatch the Officer in Function and the distinguished Rectors to go without delay to Monseigneur le Protecteur in order to assure him of the immediate execution of his orders and to inquire of him his pleasure regarding further orders."[6]

"Today Wednesday the 8th of March 1690, the Academy being met together in Extraordinary General Assembly by order of Monseigneur le Protecteur of the Academy, which the Company received pursuant to the decree of the last Assembly of the 4th of this month. About half-post four of the afternoon the Academy called upon Messrs Desjardins and de Sève, Rectors, and Messrs Regnaudin and Paillet, Professors. In the company of Monsieur de la Chapelle, all mounted the stairs and entered the Assembly where Monsieur Coypel, acting as Rector in lieu of Monsieur Le Brun, said on the Company's behalf that it had respectfully obeyed the King's wishes and had joyfully and with one voice carried out the orders of our distinguished Protector, by receiving him in the aforementioned positions, offices and ranks, and that it thereupon requested him to take his seat.

"Taking his seat, Monsieur Mignard gave thanks for the honour he had received and assured those present that he would faithfully serve the King in the offices with which His Majesty had honoured him, that he would faithfully observe all statutes and regulations, that he would submit his ideas for the deliberations of the Council, and that he would always maintain with zeal and honour the unity and peace of the Academy, both by his efforts and by his example."[6]

On the first of March the King "appointed Sieur Mignard to the office and post of his First Painter, vacant through the death of the aforementioned Sieur Le Brun, desiring . . . that he receive the same honours, authority, prerogatives, pre-eminences, immunities, liberties, wages," and on the 4th of March the Academy, paying "no heed to the ordinary procedures and what is specified in the statutes," grants Mignard "the post of Academician,

the office of Rector, and the rank of Chancellor and Director of the Company." On the 8th of March 1690 Mignard took his place and one month later the seals were handed to him.

Le Brun has passed on. Mignard holds all the offices that had been his; however he is not director of the Gobelins factory. But this is not enough. The very memory of the dead Le Brun must be done away with. "Mignard having become the King's First Painter, through Monsieur Le Brun's death, and wishing to give his portrait to the Academy, in his capacity of permanent director, he asked Rigaud to paint it. This portrait hangs in the main room of the Royal Academy."[7] These particulars are given in an abridged life of Rigaud that the latter sent to Cosimo III, Grand Duke of Tuscany. Mignard's gesture is a repetition of Le Brun's: Rigaud painted Mignard's portrait as Largillière painted Le Brun's, and thanks to this, on the 30th of March 1686, Largillière was received at the Academy as a portrait and historical painter.

Mignard dies.

"One picture 7 feet high by 6½.
"Portrait of Monsieur Mignard (Pierre) born at Troyes in Champagne, lifesize, seated, drawing in a portfolio he holds in his left hand and rests on his knee. On the table before him are a few small antique figures and some drawings, and on the floor a marble bust and various instruments used by painters.
"After Monsieur Le Brun's death, the King having conferred upon Monsieur Mignard the office of his First Painter, Mignard came to the Academy on the 5th of March 1690 and, pursuant to His Majesty's order, was accepted as an Academician, and at the same time was elected Rector, Chancellor and Director, all posts that Monsieur Le Brun had held there.
"This picture is a gift that the Countess of Feuquières, Mignard's daughter, presented to the Academy on the 28th of September 1696."[8]

This portrait of Mignard by himself is Le Brun's portrait, effaced and negated.

Le Brun sits in a velvet armchair upholstered with braid; he crosses his legs. Presumably he is in his private apartment if we judge by the shoes he is wearing and the full coat covering him, one heavy fold of which falls on the carved elbow-rest of the armchair. In his left hand lying at rest he holds paint-brushes. His right, palm open, moves very slightly towards the canvas on the easel behind him, *The Conquest of the Franche-Comté*. On the table, placed on the carpet, a fold of which falls to the floor and breaks on the floor tiles, are some unrolled, unfolded prints one of which has a torn white border. There are also two statuettes, a gladiator fighting, and some god, athlete or handsome young man. On the floor behind the armchair is a marble or plaster head resting at an angle on a book, some folded papers, a portfolio from which a pair of compasses hang, and a two-hemisphere map of the world. The objects lying about on the table and the floor, the brushes in his hand, all imply a studio. The studio of the King's First Painter in some room of the palace, as one may see from the flat fluted column and the heavy draperies drawn behind the painter.

The portrait is a copy.

Nothing in this layout differs from that of the Mignard self-portrait.

Nothing changes, not even the procedures. Just as Largillière in 1684 doubtless copied Le Brun's self-portrait for Cosimo III. In both works Le Brun wears on his chest, suspended on a cord, the portrait the King himself gave him in 1667, an oval medallion set with diamonds worn under the half-open lace collar.[9] Mignard's own self-portrait is the replica of his self-portrait for the collection of the Grand Dukes of Tuscany, engraved in 1690 by Vermelen.

We see on the table a pencil, rolled up papers, no doubt drawings, or sketches, or prints. And books: what Trajan's column indicates Mignard's nickname of "The Roman"? There are two statuettes, Diana and Venus. On the floor is a palette with brushes bunched together and stuck in the thumbhole. In a line with a maulstick, leaning against a book is a portfolio, and there is a rolled-up sheet of paper against the temple and beard of an antique head. Further back on the floor is a bust. This bust represents Catherine Mignard, his daughter. "People noticed that when he had to depict Virtues or Goddesses, he often gave them his daughter's face and form. But as she is a person of rare beauty, we need not find it strange that he used her to embellish these works."[10] "Jules de Pas, Count of Feuquières, who fell in love with Catherine Mignard, daughter of the celebrated Mignard, nicknamed the Roman, married her. She was one of the most beautiful and pleasant ladies of her time and she had numerous love affairs, something that often happens to such fine beauties."[11] What more need one say of Catherine Mignard?

Mignard is at work. Mignard is drawing in his private apartments, the apartments of the King's First Painter. Behind the armchair one sees the same flat fluted column, with, in the corner, the tassels and cords of a curtain loop. He wears a full-cut embroidered dressing gown and a black ribbon wound tightly round his shirt sleeve; it is called a "gallant," and knotted as it is at his wrist as close as possible to his hand, emphasizes its whiteness.

Behind the table, framed on a sculpted column, of which the top right hand section is concealed by the folds of the draperies falling from the ceiling, a picture is in evidence. It may be the rough-out for some frescos in the dome of the Val-de-Grâce church. By this work Mignard challenges Le Brun.

Pierre Mignard: *Self-Portrait, late 17th century*

Nicolas de Largillière: *Charles Le Brun, the King's First Painter, 1684*
Reception piece at the Academy, 1686

"The principal works he has produced since his return to France are for the dome of the Val-de-Grâce, which is the largest fresco painting in Europe," writes Charles Perrault in a book on the famous men of France in the seventeenth century.[10] The glory of the elect depicted on the Val-de-Grâce dome is one episode in the long-standing rivalry between the King's First Painters. Petitions, lampoons and pamphlets, one of them anonymous, all bear witness to the conflict between them. On the 23rd of March 1669 Pierre Le Petit published a quarto edition of Molière's poem *La Gloire du Val-de-Grâce*, illustrated with vignettes and a tailpiece by Mignard.

One passage in praise of Mignard's fresco reads:

"Though your glory will set rival brushes to work and spur them to emulation, your Val-de-Grâce dome will remain the wonder of our time, and from the ends of the earth will attract inquiring and knowing minds to this splendid place.

"And this stately dome is an open school where this work, acting as the voice, lays down the sovereign laws of your great art. It clearly sets forth the three noble parts[12] which make up the matching beauties of a picture, and which thus brought together illustrate the best talents given to the world by the master painters."

But Molière's poem is not just a defence of the dome frescos, not just a eulogy of Mignard, it is also an attack on Le Brun, as the lines already quoted remind us:

"Great men, Colbert, are poor courtiers,
Little inclined to truckling duties.

Who gives himself to court life is lost to art."

Some time later appeared an anonymous poem entitled *La Coupe du Val-de-Grâce* (The Dome of the Val-de-Grâce). The preface to the new, Anonimiana edition of 1700 states: "It may not be irrelevant to inform the reader that the first sixty or eighty lines of this poem have the same rhymes as the opening lines of Molière's *Val-de-Grâce*, and that, since this excellent actor had only written his poem in order to praise Mignard, the lady who produced this critical response to it only did so in order to curry favour with Monsieur de Colbert, who was the patron and protector of Le Brun, Mignard's rival and competitor."

Elisabeth Sophie Chéron, a painter and one of the few women to be admitted at the time to membership of the Royal Academy, and also a poet, who in 1699 was honoured by the Academy of Padua with the pen name of Erato,[13] was in fact the author of this latter poem in defence of Le Brun, which only remained anonymous for a short time.

She set the dome speaking, or rather confessing, and into its mouth put these words:

"All my beauty is only a pretence, seen through by any man skilled in art... If Raphael the true painter had treated this subject, he would have refrained from all that displeases us here."

No understatement here: the lady speaks her mind freely.

In the rest of the poem she makes it plain that for her Mignard, in his Val-de-Grâce frescos, proved himself more of a courtier than a painter: "Tone,

Elisabeth Sophie Chéron:
Self-Portrait. Reception piece at the Academy, 1672

Medals and a hunting picture
or
Portrait of an office

"At the Academy of Painting and Sculpture hangs a picture six feet high by five wide.

"It represents a huntsman resting in an open landscape, while on the terrace in the foreground lie a good many pieces of game. He is leaning on his gun and is accompanied by several dogs, of which he is petting the nearest one. This is the painter's own portrait.

"By Alexandre François Desportes, animal painter, born at Champigneule, near Grand-Pré, in Champagne. Admitted to the Academy on the 1st of August 1699, elected councillor on the 17th of March 1704."[1]

On the 3rd of August 1748 this artist's son, Claude François Desportes, read before the Academy a memoir of his father's life. In it he said: "His reception piece, in which he portrayed himself as a huntsman with dogs and game, is regarded by this company as one of the finest pictures now decorating its assembly hall."[2] After this proud statement, he added: "In 1702 he painted for Louis XIV two very fine hounds pointing at pheasants and partridges in a charming landscape. Thereafter he painted one after another all the hounds which the King subsequently owned. Indeed it was his wont to accompany the King on his game shooting, with a small notebook in which, on the spot, he drew the hounds in action, in various attitudes, from which the King would chose, always with taste, the particular attitudes which he preferred to the others."[2] Desportes, to whom Louis XIV assigned an apartment in the Louvre, decorated the menagerie at Versailles and painted to the King's order the rare animals it contained. Through the king Desportes was a huntsman, for the king he was a painter. His self-portrait combines the two, as required by the king.

"In the second hall where are ordinarily held the assemblies" of the Royal Academy of Painting and Sculpture, hung "a portrait of Antoine Coypel, director of the Academy, painted by himself and presented by him to the Academy."[1] Seated in an

masses, values, impasto, are all meaningless words for him, for in his dome not one of them finds a place."[14]

The portrait of the King's First Painter by himself, this self-portrait by Mignard, presented to the Academy by his handsome daughter the Countess of Feuquières, who sat for the Virtues and Goddesses in his other pictures, effaces and negates the portrait of Le Brun, the King's previous First Painter, by Largillière. The dead Mignard displaces and dispatches Le Brun.

"When Mignard was stricken with the illness from which he died, he was completing a picture of St. Luke, the patron saint of painters, in which he portrayed himself holding a palette and brushes. There is even a little bit of carpet that he left unfinished."[10]

Mignard died on the 30th of May 1695, five years after Le Brun. He was interred in the Paris church of Les Jacobins Saint Honoré.

François Desportes:
Portrait of the Artist as a Huntsman
Reception piece at the Academy, 1699

armchair, his left hand resting on the carved arm-rest, and wearing a loose coat over which the curls of his wig fall, the painter holds propped against his leg a bound volume stamped with gold letters and fleur-de-lys designs. At the top of the spine is a crown. Beneath it the title reads: MÉDAILLES LOUIS LE GRAND.

"Men of indifferent ability in the Fine Arts think themselves sufficiently rewarded by the man who satisfies their interest. Those who seek distinction in the Fine Arts aim at a nobler reward. They want plaudits, more than they receive and more perhaps than they deserve."[3] Coypel was one of those who wanted the nobler reward of general recognition and approval. He got them, being ennobled not so much for his painting as for the care he bestowed on the king's medals.

Coypel's office was to look after the medals, as Desportes' was to go shooting with the king.

Their portrait in each case is the portrait of an office in the king's service.

Studio

A work of art is a corner of creation seen through a temperament.

Emile Zola, *Mes Haines*

1870. Bazille is holding open house. In a studio where the view from the window, with its green serge curtains drawn to one side, gives on the roofs and façades of Paris buildings. The angle of view shows the studio to be at the top of the house. The heating is provided by a stove working at full blast to keep the place warm, despite the height of the ceiling, beneath which is a loggia reached by a wooden staircase on the left. Bazille is holding open house. For a client? A critic? A painter friend? In front of the canvas standing on an easel, on which Bazille, still holding his palette, was no doubt work-

ing, are two men, one of them wearing a round hat. They are commenting on, perhaps praising the still unfinished painting. On the walls are pictures, both framed and unframed, and a palette. People are having a discussion. Someone is playing the piano. Music, words, painting. It was this kind of studio, built with large windows facing north so that the light would be evenly distributed from sunrise to sunset, that brought to an end the history of the painter painting himself at his place of work. For only twenty or thirty years had the studio been this kind of place with a loggia and large windows.

For centuries the studio was a room, an ordinary room in the house or apartments. In Italy it was a workshop or *bottega*. Or it might be a room in a palace, or some large disused convent room. (David

painted *The Coronation of Napoleon* in the disused church of the Collège de Cluny.)[1] In the eighteenth century painters used to live in the Louvre in the wing of the palace giving on the banks of the Seine. The Louvre was also the seat of the Royal Academy of Painting and Sculpture which collected the rents for the shops built at the sides of the palace itself, along the so-called Waterside Gallery. Twenty-six artists lived there in rooms separated by partitions from the royal palace. Among them were Greuze and Fragonard.[2] The Revolution brought about the invasion of the palace where, until then, residence required royal authorization; this had been the case since the letters patent of 1608 signed by Henry IV and confirmed by Louis XIV in 1671. On the 3rd of Fructidor, Year IX, a decree evicted some of the artists living in the palace; and a second decree of eviction was enacted on the 18th of May 1806. The latter decree granted a pension of from 500 to 1000 francs by way of indemnity.[1]

In the seventeenth century Velázquez lived in the apartments of a deceased prince in the Alcázar. And Rembrandt painted in one room of his Amsterdam house. It was only from the sixteenth century onwards that the painter portrayed himself as a painter, palette and brushes in hand. And it was only in the seventeenth century that in Holland the theme of the artist at work in his studio was to be repeated with multiple variations. To portray oneself as a painter in the studio was not debasing oneself in the diligent, hard-working society of Holland. This would have been the case in Italy at the same era, since the Italian patrons were titled people, whereas in Holland the painter's clients were bourgeois like himself, who may well have belonged to the same militia. And the theme of the painter in his studio was to broaden out still further: the studio gets cluttered with various models of objects, casts, sculptures, and also visitors wandering about or posing. The portrait has become a genre scene.

Perhaps the self-portrait is always an implicit acknowledgment of the painter's place of work: the cap worn pulled down over the ears in the Quattrocento implies the cold church where the painter is working on a fresco and the place is still damp from the plaster applied that very morning. The bulky

Jan Vermeer: *The Artist's Studio or Allegory of Painting, c. 1666*

velvet dressing-gowns worn by the King's First Painters such as Le Brun or Mignard were evidence that they lived in apartments in the Palace, as the silk embroidered jackets which adorned Goya spoke of the Court – that is the Spanish Court after it had abandoned the austere mourning imposed by Philip IV, to which Velázquez submitted.

The space where the painter painted, whether a room or a studio, the clothes he wore, his hair-style and all the objects around him such as models of objects, works of art or the presence of visitors, are all of import. The painter paints himself. He paints himself at the place where he does his painting. And nothing is left to chance.

Is he anonymous, the painter we see from behind painting in Vermeer's studio? An odd kind of anonymity. The light coming from a window behind the heavy looped-back curtain illumines from the left the woman posing: Clio crowned with laurels. And all Vermeer's interiors are similarly illumined, except for *The Lace-Maker*. There can be no doubt! Here is Vermeer in his own studio around 1666, painting an allegory.

◁ Frédéric Bazille: *The Artist's Studio, 1870*

William Hogarth: *Self-Portrait (Hogarth painting the Comic Muse)*, *1758*

Comedy
or
From one mirror to another

It hath been thought a vast commendation of a painter to say his figures seem to breathe; but surely it is a much greater and nobler applause that they appear to think.[1]

Fielding

William Hogarth, seated in an armchair, wearing a red cap that dangles on the back of his almost bald head, is examining the canvas standing on the easel in front of him. No doubt he is judging the chalk sketch for it still held in his right hand. It depicts Comedy beside a column, considering a mask that she turns toward her with her left hand; under her right arm she carries a thick book. Hogarth is perhaps about to stretch out his hand in order to correct one line or another, or it may be

that he is going to put down the piece of chalk and start painting. He holds a palette all prepared in his left hand and grasps a fistful of paint brushes.

"My picture is my stage, and men and women are my players, who by means of certain actions and gestures are to exhibit a dumb show," writes Hogarth.[2] Thus a self-portrait in which the painter himself is at work on a sketch of Comedy herself is equivalent to painting a manifesto declaring that one is a painter of the theatre. It is painting in one mirror, another mirror.

"All the world's a stage,
And all the men and women merely players:
They have their exits and their entrances;
And one man in his time plays many parts."[3]

"The purpose of playing, whose end, both first and now, was and is, to hold, as t'were, the mirror up to nature; to show virtue her own feature, scorn her own image, and the very age and body of the time his form and pressure."[4]

These manifestos stem from Shakespeare, over whose bound works, together with those of Swift and Milton, stands the oval portrait of Hogarth, another manifesto dated 1745. This self-portrait of Hogarth is the first one he painted. In the foreground sits Trump, a pug who reappears in picture after picture, since the death of Pugg which was announced in *The Craftsman* of the 5th of September 1730. On the left there is a tilted palette bearing no trace of paint. Resting on this palette is a thin stem rising and curving, underlined by shadow. What this line echoed by shadow means is spelled out in a text:

The LINE of BEAUTY
and GRACE

These words are written on the palette, the first line in yellow letters, the second in red. Between this Line of Beauty and Grace and the thumb-hole, in the same yellow lettering, are the signature and the date: W. H. 1745. This line is the central idea of the theory that Hogarth was to expound in *The Analysis of Beauty* in 1753. This signature in the form of initials was the one he was to use in the future; it even appeared on the painter's carriage.

The portrait of Hogarth placed on the volume of Shakespeare's works and Hogarth in his armchair sketching Comedy on a canvas: this is the Hogarth who decided to "compose pictures on canvas similar to representations on the stage, and farther hope that they will be tried by the same test, and criticized by the same criterion."[5] After all, "Life's but a walking shadow, a poor player, that struts and frets his hour upon the stage, and then is heard no more; it is a tale told by an idiot, full of sound and fury, signifying nothing."[6]

William Hogarth: *Self-Portrait with his Pug Dog, 1745*

The eye deceived

In Chapter VII headed "On the Essence of Painting," in his seventeenth-century treatise on "The Idea of the Perfect Painter," André Félibien wrote: "We have said that painting was an art which by means of Drawing and Colour imitates all visible objects on a flat surface. This is more or less the way in which all who have spoken of it have defined it, and until the present day no one has seen fit to revise this definition."[1] Dürer's own definition was no different: "Painting is the ability to represent on a flat surface an object, any one you choose, from among all the visible objects in existence."[2]

This definition, which at the outset of the eighteenth century no one had sought to revise, was not to change for a long time to come. Painting is re-presenting. And this re-presentation has as its aim to deceive the eye, to deceive any eye. "It is said that, in his youth, Giotto one day painted a fly so realistically on the nose of a face started by Cimabue, that this master, when he resumed work on it, tried to chase the fly away with his hand before realizing his mistake."[3] Cimabue's mistake, his eye deceived by a fly of Giotto's making, is only an anecdote recounted to us; Giotto's fly is Parrhasios' veil. This veil painted by Parrhasios challenged Zeuxis' eye, Zeuxis who had misled the birds' eyes with his grapes; this veil haunted painting and haunted painters. To be a painter is to deceive the eye like this; with his fly, Giotto seeks to be Parrhasios and Cimabue is Zeuxis.

Diderot's eye, when he was visiting the Salon in 1759, was deceived by a Chardin painting of the return from the hunt: "It's always nature and truth; you'd take the bottles by the neck if you were thirsty; the peaches and grapes whet the appetite and make you want to reach for them."[4] Zeuxis' grapes are Chardin's grapes; Zeuxis misled the birds' vision, and that year Chardin deceived a philosopher's eye; and that same philosopher, looking at another Chardin four years later cried out: "You see, that porcelain vase really is porcelain; those olives are really separated from the eye by the water they're floating in; you just have to pick up those biscuits and eat them; cut open the Seville orange and squeeze it; take the glass of wine and drink it; peel the fruit; cut the meat pie with your knife. Ah, my friend, you can spit on Apelles' curtain [does it matter if Parrhasios' curtain is erroneously attributed to Apelles?] and on Zeuxis' grapes. An impatient artist is readily deceived and animals are bad judges of painting. Haven't we seen the birds in the king's garden breaking their heads against the worst of painted vistas? But it's you, it's I whom Chardin will mislead whenever he wants to."[5]

Chardin deceives the eye of philosophers and encyclopaedists like Diderot and Grimm. Their eyes have to surrender. Evidence in paint imposes this capitulation, this surrender. Painting is deliberately a snare in which the eye is caught.

"Near the theatre in Milan, in a stable that is today dilapidated and in ruins, Bramantino painted some stable-boys grooming horses. One of the boys looked so alive and was so cleverly painted that a horse, believing him to be real, kicked out at him time and again."[6]

This horse that lashed out at a painted groom proclaims Bramantino to be Apelles' equal, Apelles who is an obsession throughout all the history of painting. Again in 1829, Paillot de Montabert in his treatise on painting tells us that "Apelles painted such a good likeness of Alexander that Bucephalus neighed when he saw his master's portrait." The kick of an anonymous horse is quite as valid as Bucephalus' neigh. Was it this neigh of Bucephalus that was the origin of the privileges Alexander granted Apelles? "Apelles often painted Alexander's portrait, and since this monarch did not find it seemly to allow his image to be profaned by ignorant hands, he issued a decree by which he forbade all painters to portray him with the sole exception of Apelles."[7]

It was because of this likeness that Apelles came to be Alexander's protégé. Thus, seeking to be the Apelles of one's time is to claim the ability to deceive the eye as he did, and as a reward to claim the same patronage and privileges from the great. And he who makes of a painter the Apelles of his time, at a single stroke, makes of himself the Alexander of his time. Charles the Fifth, who appointed Titian "painter in ordinary"[8] to the emperor, the sole painter with the privilege of painting his portrait, was not ignorant of the metaphor implied by the privilege he granted: it made Titian Apelles and Charles the Fifth Alexander.

This likeness that deceives the eye has its price. In France during the Second Empire a painter listed his charges as follows: "A perfect likeness: 20 francs. A fair likeness: 15 francs. A family likeness: 10 francs. People wearing medals: 2 francs extra."[9]

Painting is an art which imitates all visible objects on a flat surface, a definition that no one found it necessary to revise until...

One statement is sufficient to show that this definition has been refuted. Braque said: "*Ce qui est entre la pomme et l'assiette se peint aussi*": What there is *between* the apple and the plate must also be painted.[10]

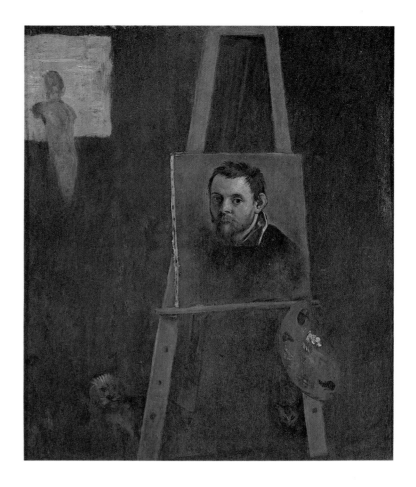

The painter painted

In a studio,, standing on an easel from which a colour-laden palette is suspended, a portrait: the portrait of the painter by himself.

A painter looks away from the portrait he is finishing, his hand resting against the maulstick which cuts diagonally across the portrait of a young woman. This portrait is that of the painter by herself. This portrait of Bernardino Campi painting the portrait of Sofonisba Anguissola is the portrait of Sofonisba Anguissola by Sofonisba Anguissola. This self-portrait was painted as a token of gratitude, for it was in Campi's studio in Cremona that both Sofonisba and her sister Elena learned to paint. To portray oneself being painted by the man who taught one painting is to declare that, if one has become a painter, it is thanks to that master.

Hogarth's oval portrait standing on the works of Shakespeare, Milton and Swift thereby declares that it is based on those works.

Carracci's completed, unframed portrait stands on the easel. Here is a painter who after portraying himself has painted a picture of the portrait. To take this step suggests that he wished to be more than a painter, he wished to be an expression of painting itself, of painting pure and simple. To be a painter and to paint a picture of one's own portrait is to re-experience painting through painting alone and to distil oneself into a work of art. Annibale Carracci ceases to be and only Carraccis remain.

Sofonisba Anguissola: *Bernardino Campi painting the Portrait of Sofonisba Anguissola, c. 1560*

Portrait of the gaze: eye to eye

Accessories are not to be taken lightly.[1]

Diderot

Nothing matters more in a self-portrait than the painter's gaze. Palette, turban, cap, brushes, easel, frock coat, straw hat, medals, toga, maulstick, satin waistcoat, grog-blossoms, wig, short hair, long hair, all this is of little account. It is the expression of the eyes that matters. The gaze is the very first thing to be painted; the features of a face are merely trappings like all the rest. (La Tour resigned himself to framing his gaze with his features and his roughed-out face remains a mask, another accessory.) To paint oneself is to look oneself full in the eyes and plumb their depths. To paint oneself is to paint the act of seeing. The eyes are the identity. (When identity is lost in death, the eyelids are closed.)

From the motif

A landscape painter needs to know a great many things. An understanding of perspective, architecture and human and animal anatomy are not enough; in addition he must have some knowledge of botany and mineralogy.[1]

Goethe

Surrounded by undergrowth and seated on a fallen tree trunk, Jacob More is painting. He is in shirt-sleeves and waistcoat, his coat and hat have been laid down on a gnarled root and his walking-stick leans against it. There is no easel, no box of paints. He has a canvas resting on his knee and holds in his left hand a palette and a few brushes. The painter is working on a landscape in the variegated shadow of russet foliage.

More has been living in Rome since 1773. His nickname is based on an anagram: people call him More of Rome. (And presumably this particular nickname is a deliberate reminder of the memory of the Moor of Venice, not that More is an Othello,

3

On horseback

In 1758-1759, in the company of Mary Spencer, by whom he had a son, George Stubbs spent eighteen months on a farm in Lincolnshire. Day after day he dissected horses. In 1766 he published his classic *Anatomy of the Horse*. In 1790 the *Turf Review* ordered a series of portraits from him: portraits of the finest race horses. Some years later this series was to be engraved.

Between the time when Stubbs was preparing his *Anatomy of the Horse*, and the time when the *Turf Review* ordered the series of portraits of the finest race horses of the day, Stubbs painted his own portrait: wearing a three-cornered hat, George Stubbs is on horseback.

4

1. Maurice Quentin de La Tour:
   Self-Portrait or Mask, c. 1742

2. Rembrandt: *Self-Portrait at the Easel, 1660*

3. Jacob More: *Self-Portrait painting in the Woods, 1783*

4. George Stubbs: *Self-Portrait on a White Hunter, 1782*

but rather for Shakespeare and England.) From 1771 on, at the Society of Artists in London, he exhibited a number of landscapes, those falls of Clyde, Stonebyres, Corra Linn and Bonnington which made him famous throughout Europe and won him the admiration of Goethe and Prince Borghese.

The self-portrait he is working on speaks neither of England nor Italy. But it proclaims a will and a fact. More is painting out of doors, More is painting directly from the motif. This portrait confirms that the landscapes have not been recreated in the studio from rough drawings or sketches. I am painting out of doors.

Goya at the Spanish court
or
The rise of a new dynasty

The king's First Secretary of State, His Excellency Don José Moñino, Count of Floridablanca, stands erect, the back of his left hand on his hip above the broad ribbon of a decoration worn across his chest. He holds a monocle near the canvas that Francisco Goya is showing him, but does not look at the painter. It is half-past ten; this is the hour shown by the dial of the gilt clock on a table covered by a carpet to His Excellency's right. There are also documents and plans, and others are leaning

against the tablecloth which reaches down to the floor, among them a plan of the Aragon Canal. At floor level, on the carpet, there is a bound book and lying in front of the painter's foot, an unfolded sheet of paper.

> Señor
> Fran.co Goya

is written on this sheet. We also find, at the bottom of the plan of the Aragon Canal:

> AL EXC.MO SEÑO[R] FLORIDA BLANCA
> AÑO 1783

And finally on the book lying on the floor: PALO PRAC DE L PINTUR 2-3 (which should be read as: Palomino, *Práctica de la Pintura*).

The signature, the dedication, the reference.

Since 1777 the Count of Floridablanca has been the First Secretary of State to His Majesty Charles III. "Don José Moñino, attorney general of my Council of Castile, is very well informed about everything, and he is a good royalist," wrote the king when his minister was appointed. It was at the beginning of 1783 that the Count ordered his portrait from Goya, who had been a member of the Royal Academy of San Fernando for three years. Goya wrote to his friend Martín Zapater about it: was a career at the Court about to begin for him? It was through Count Floridablanca that Goya had obtained his first royal order in 1781: *The Miracle of St. Bernardino of Siena preaching in the Presence of King Alfonso V*, for the Madrid Church of San Francisco el Grande, only just completed.

Don Juan Martín de Goicoechea persuaded Floridablanca to agree that the order for the portrait should go to Goya. And Goya countersigned it with a likeness of himself, this being the first work commissioned from him by the Court.

Goya presents his portrait to the Minister. And then he waited for the Minister to intervene, to become his patron at the Court. Goya waited. "Dear Friend, there is no news. Up to now there is more silence concerning my relations with Señor Moñino than before I painted his portrait."[1] Nothing; and time was passing. "Everyone is surprised that there has been no result from the Minister of State after this picture, which he liked so much."[1] Continuing silence. "If nothing comes from that quarter, there is nothing more to be hoped for, and when one has hoped for so much, the disappointment is all the greater."[2] There was to be nothing but silence.

During the summer of 1783, the Infante Don Luís de Borbón, brother of Charles III, arranged for Goya to come to Arenas de San Pedro at the foot of the Sierra de Gredos and paint his portrait together with his family. The King's First Minister had failed to open the doors of the Court for Goya: would the King's brother do so? In the summer of 1783, in August and September, Goya painted the portrait of the Infante in the midst of his family and servants. Seated at a table the Infante is playing

Francisco Goya: *The Count of Floridablanca, with Goya presenting the Count's Portrait to him, 1783*

Francisco Goya: *The Family of the Infante Don Luis de Borbón, with Goya painting them, 1783*

cards; behind the table his wife, Doña María Teresa de Vallabriga, is in an armchair having her hair arranged. The Infante had married her in 1776 after renouncing his position as a church dignitary; till then he had been Cardinal-Archbishop of Toledo and Seville, and prominent at Court. Beside them here are their three children: Don Luís María de Borbón y Vallabriga, later to become the Cardinal-Archbishop of Toledo; Doña María Teresa, who was to marry Godoy; and little Doña María Luisa in the arms of her nurse; she became the wife of the Duke of San Fernando. And also Goya, who seated behind the Infante on a sort of packing-case and seen from the rear, is starting to work on a canvas, still blank, placed on the ground against his easel. Projected shadows are all that can be seen on the canvas. In his left hand Goya holds a palette laid out with colours, a few brushes and a maulstick. In his right he has a chalk-holder and is turning towards María Teresa whose face he is studying over

the Infante's shoulder. Goya is embarking on his portrait; Goya is embarking on his career at the Court. But this royal patron was to die in 1785.

Floridablanca had done nothing for him; the Infante, the King's brother, could no longer do anything. But Goya's career was starting. On the 18th of March 1785 he was appointed vice-principal of the painting class at the Academy. At last, in 1786, he was appointed Painter to the King. But King Charles III died on the 25th of June 1786. Charles IV succeeded him. Goya could only wait. Meanwhile he remained the King's Painter with 15,000 reals a year. To Zapater he wrote: "*Martín mio, ya soy Pintor del Rey con quince mil reales!*"

In April 1789 Don Francisco Goya was named "Painter of the Chamber, with all the rights that this position enjoys today." From then on, Don Francisco Goya was addressed as Your Excellency. On the 4th of October 1795 His Excellency was elected director of painting at the Academy of San

Francisco Goya:
The Family of Charles IV,
with Goya painting them, 1800-1801

Fernando. In 1797 when he resigned from this post he was granted the title of Honorary Director as a tribute to his "distinguished merits."

Finally, on the 31st of October 1799, with a tax-free income of 50,000 reals a year and 500 ducats for the upkeep of a carriage, His Excellency was appointed First Painter of the Chamber by a decree from the king's minister Urquijo.

It was therefore he who received the order to paint the king and his family. Goya was to do the portrait at Aranjuez where the royal family was spending this spring of 1800. Four carriages were used to transport the stretchers and canvases. In late May and early June Goya made ten portrait studies in preparation for *The Family of Charles IV.*

The royal family is gathered together in one of the rooms at Aranjuez. On the right, the Infanta María Luisa is holding in her arms Don Carlos Luís, not yet one year old. (Goya conceals the fact that this Infante suffers from a curvature of the spine and has one shoulder higher than the other.) Next to her, wearing a red coat, is her husband Don Luís de Borbón, Prince of Parma. Behind his shoulder, in profile, is the king's elder sister, the Infanta Carlota Joaquina. At her side is the Infante Don Antonio Pascual, brother of Charles IV who stands in front of them holding the hand of the little Infante Don Francisco de Paula Antonio. Queen María Luisa also holds the Infante's hand. Her white gold-spangled dress with broad golden skirts is no doubt one of her numerous fineries that even the ambassadors felt they must report on to Madrid. Alguier, the French Ambassador, wrote of her: "At the age of fifty she has the pretensions and coquetry scarcely to be pardoned in a young and pretty woman. Her expenditure on jewels and fin-

ery is enormous and it is rare that a courrier from an ambassador arrives without bringing her two or three gowns." The Queen puts her right hand round the Infanta María Isabel's shoulder. Beside them, a princess with her face averted. Who is it?

Behind this princess, her temple marked with lupus, is the Infanta María Josefa, the king's sister. In front of her, wearing a blue coat, Ferdinand, Prince of Asturias: "A bewildered husband, idle, deceitful, mean, sly and not even a man physically. It is a shame when at the age of eighteen one responds to nothing: neither commands nor persuasion have any effect upon him... The Prince does nothing, doesn't read, doesn't write, doesn't think... Nothing... And this is deliberate because they want him to be an idiot. He makes me blush at his coarseness to people." This pen portrait is by María Antonina, daughter of the Queen of Naples, Maria Carolina. It describes the future Ferdinand VII. Behind him, putting his hands on Ferdinand's hips is his young brother Don Carlos María Isidro.

And lastly, behind all of them, in the shadow of an upright canvas of which only the reverse side and stretchers are visible, is His Excellency, the First Painter of the Chamber, Don Francisco Goya. His position is that of Velázquez. His *Family of Charles IV* is *Las Meninas* reversed. Philip IV is posing opposite Velázquez and the royal couple's reflection appears in the mirror behind the painter. Charles IV and his family, with Goya behind them, are posing in front of a mirror... And Goya's position is Velázquez' position: the First Painter of the Chamber stands in the place formerly occupied by the Grand Marshal of the Palace. A new dynasty is being contrived.

Allusive headgear

In Paris, in 1825, Madame Hortense Haudebourt-Lescot painted a self-portrait. Her arms folded across her chest, she holds a pencil in her right hand. Her face has begun to thicken as she reaches her forties, an active and versatile artist showing every year at the Salon. Around her neck, left bare by her dress and her chemise, she wears a chain, with rings hanging from it, reminiscent of those worn by the heroes of Ossian – an eighteenth-century fashion still in vogue? On her head, a heavy beret of black velvet.

Are this northern beret and chain perhaps intended as a tribute to Rembrandt the Dutchman? (Soon afterwards Madame Haudebourt-Lescot was to paint with that careful attention to detail said to be typical of the Dutch.)

Standing, with palette and brushes Madame Elisabeth Vigée-Lebrun looks at us with an open countenance, about to relax into a smile. She wears a straw hat with flowers and a feather. "This admirable picture represents one of Rubens's women. Its major effect lies in the two kinds of light, partly ordinary daylight, partly sunshine. The brighter parts are lit by the sun and what I must call the shadows, for want of a better word, are in daylight. This picture delights me; to the point that I painted my own portrait in Brussels seeking to achieve the same effect. I painted myself wearing a straw hat, a feather, and a garland of wild flowers, and holding a palette."[1] She claims, then, that Rubens inspired her. In this self-portrait is she taking up the challenge or paying tribute? Or both?

Hortense Haudebourt-Lescot:
Self-Portrait with Pencil, 1825

Elisabeth Vigée-Lebrun:
Self-Portrait with Straw Hat and Palette, 1782

Jean-Etienne Liotard: *Self-Portrait as the Turkish Painter, 1744*

Luis Meléndez: *Self-Portrait with Drawing of a Male Nude, 1746*

Jean-Baptiste Siméon Chardin: *Self-Portrait
with an Éyeshade, 1775*

Rembrandt: *Self-Portrait with Gorget, c. 1633-1634*

1866: Courbet is wearing a helmet with the visor lifted. Courbet is smiling. Courbet as a knight . . . is this self-mockery? Is it a masquerade? Is it a reference to Rembrandt wearing a helmet in 1634, or to other self-portraits of Rembrandt in armour?

Overbeck, like Wilhelm von Schadow and Thorvaldsen, wears a beret. For these young men in Italy, this old-fashioned beret typical of German artists is the affirmation of their patriotism.

Meléndez has tied up his hair with a *panuello de cabeza*. A sort of kerchief, this popular headgear was soon to become typical of the *mayos*, the dandies of Madrid who strolled by the Manzanares. Was Meléndez' kerchief meant to stress his kinship with the people of Madrid?

Liotard was "nicknamed the Turkish Painter," as he tells us himself in the self-portrait he sent in to the portrait collection of the Grand Dukes of Tuscany. And he proves himself a Turk by the fur cap he is wearing, similar to the one worn by Antoine de Favray thirty years later.

Chardin wears a white headcloth edged with pink, like a turban knotted in front. And an eyeshade, green and rigid, held by a cord that we must imagine laced behind the head.

Goya stands in front of a bright glass window wearing a top hat. On the brim of it, set in clothes pins, are candles. The glass window and this crown of candles are a counterpoint of light. One painter's eyeshade and the other's top hat are their studio secrets.

Tribute, challenge, reminder, secret, the painter's headgear is not only a cap, a beret, a toque, a straw hat or a turban, a kerchief or a top hat. The accessory speaks out. The allusion is alluvial.

Francisco Goya: *Self-Portrait painting in his Studio, 1785*

Faithful

"Monseigneur,

Having had the good fortune to admire the collection of rare masterpieces that comprises Your Highness's picture gallery, and knowing that artists were permitted to mark the occasion by contributing their self-portraits, I have taken the liberty of enjoying this privilege by offering Your Royal Highness the self-portrait I have sent to the Director of His Academy, to be submitted on my behalf as a pale tribute to the love of the arts shown by illustrious predecessors and which Your Highness cultivates with so great a distinction. This noble sentiment can but add to that feeling of profound respect with which I am..."[1]

This letter, sent from Rome on the 30th of August 1791, is signed by Elisabeth Vigée-Lebrun. The self-portrait offered by Madame Vigée-Lebrun was accepted by His Serene Highness the Grand Duke of Tuscany, Ferdinand III.

On the 19th of September 1791, the Director of the Uffizi Gallery in Florence wrote: "Madame, pursuant to the letter I had the honour to write you on the 5th of this month, I am informing you by these presents that His Royal Highness is most pleased to accept your portrait and to grant me permission to hang it in this Royal Gallery. It is with extreme pleasure that I undertake this Royal Gallery. It is with extreme pleasure that I undertake this commission, all the more so because I esteem and admire a work that may rightly be called a masterpiece of art."

Seated before the easel, she is painting. Her left hand lying on her knee is closed, with the thumb in the palette resting on her forearm on a bundle of brushes. (One of them has been dipped in a red paint of the same hue as the sash knotted at her waist.) Her black dress has lace-edged sleeves and a lace collar. She wears a light turban knotted above her right temple and some curls of brown hair hang down from it: "I wound a muslin fichu round my head."[2]

Her lips are parted and she is smiling. The brush in her right hand reaches towards the canvas before her, where we can see the outline, still undefined, pale and incomplete of a portrait. Maybe Elisabeth Vigée-Lebrun is painting between two posing sessions? Perhaps it is the sitter she turns to and is studying for a moment?

The portrait she is working on is not of herself. It is not a self-portrait she is roughing out on the canvas, despite that look which seems to be directed at a mirror. Elisabeth Vigée-Lebrun is not portraying that abyss of herself painting her own portrait. The

Elisabeth Vigée-Lebrun:
Self-Portrait at the Easel, c. 1791

Adélaïde Labille-Guiard: *Self-Portrait with Two Pupils,*
Mademoiselle Marie Gabrielle Capet and Mademoiselle Carreaux de Rosemond, 1785

portrait sketch is that of Marie-Antoinette, Queen of France.

Was she still the queen? Elisabeth Vigée-Lebrun's portrait of herself painting the queen caused Ménageot, Director of the French Academy in Rome, to write to the Count of Angiviller on the 3rd of March 1790, saying: "Madame Le Brun has just completed her portrait for the Grand Duke's Gallery in Florence; it is one of the finest things she has produced. I think she has acquired much more skill since I left Paris. This painting has amazed everyone who has seen it up to now."[3] A few months later – it was on the night of the 20th of June – the queen climbed into that too heavy coach waiting in front of a door in the Tuileries palace which La Fayette had left unguarded to enable Count Axel de Fersen to reach the queen. Her Majesty, disguised like the king as a *valet de chambre*, entered the coach. It reached Châlons five hours late and the relay horses were no longer waiting. The coach was to be halted at the barricaded bridge over the Aire at Varennes. On the 25th of June the king and the royal family were brought back to Paris: the crowd was silent, the soldiers lining the way presented their arms reversed. The monarchy was at an end. On the 27th of August 1791 the Declaration of Pillnitz threatened revolutionary France with European arms. Elisabeth Vigée-Lebrun's letter was dated the 30th of August. Two weeks later the king swore fidelity to the nation, whose constitution he had accepted. Was the queen still queen?

Elisabeth Vigée-Lebrun was an intimate of Marie-Antoinette, by then ridiculed and shut up in the Tuileries; she painted numerous portraits of her. It was to the queen that she owed her renown, and it was through the queen that she had been admitted to the Academy on the 31st of May 1783, on the same day that Adélaïde Labille-Guiard was also admitted – "Her talent takes after that of a Diana, Madame Le Brun's stems from Venus"[4] – a rival who in 1785 painted a self-portrait seated before a canvas. Shown at the Salon that same year as No. 101 in the catalogue, it was entitled: *A Picture (Portrait) of three full-length figures representing a woman in the act of painting and two pupils watching.* The latter are two young women: Mademoiselle Carreaux de Rosemond and Mademoiselle Marie Gabrielle Capet.[4] (This, as it happened, was also the surname of the royal family, and Marie-Antoinette was contemptuously referred to as "the Capet woman.")

In exile in Rome, to paint the portrait of the discredited queen at the time of the Varennes flight, and to paint this portrait for the most celebrated collection of self-portraits in Europe, is a declaration of fidelity; a determination to be faithful to her whatever the consequences.

Tumour

His hair is powdered and falls in curls over his ears. Jacques-Louis David is staring at himself in a mirror. A white cravat is wound and knotted round his neck, held, like the ruffle, by the form of the turned-down collars of waistcoats worn over each other under a morning coat with turned-down flaps. The upper lip, on the right side of the face, in the shadow, is swollen. A tumour.

His half-length brown hair is not powdered now. Seated in an armchair is Jacques-Louis David, a member of the erstwhile Academy of Painting and Sculpture. At the Convention, at the session of the 8th of August 1793, Citizen David proclaimed: "In the name of humanity, in the name of justice, for the love of art, and above all because of our love for youth, let us destroy, let us annihilate those baleful Academies that can no longer continue their existence in a free regime. As an Academician I have done my duty. Pass sentence."[1] David was a deputy representing the Department of Paris and a friend of Robespierre. At an evening meeting on the 8th of Thermidor, after re-reading a speech that Robespierre had made that same day to the Convention, David called out: "Robespierre, if you drink hemlock, I shall drink it with you!" In his 1794 self-portrait he is holding a palette in his right hand, a brush in his left. That same year he was arrested. On the 2nd of Frimaire of the Year III he writes: "Well, in one respect then shall I finally be likened to Apelles? He too was accused of conspiracy, against Ptolemy, by the painter Antiphiles, and it was then that Apelles painted his picture of Calumny. Although I do not possess his divine talent, I do have plenty of Antiphiles around me, because I still maintain with insistence that it is the artists of the Academy who continue to make accusations against me to members of the Convention of their acquaintance."[2] The upper lip, on the right side of the face, in the shadow, is swollen. A tumour.

In the 1815 portrait of David the curly hair is cut short, and there are wrinkles of age about the eyes. Pinned to the lapel of his frock coat is the Legion of Honour, with a rosette on the ribbon, immediately above the crowned medal. Jacques-Louis David, now First Painter to the imperial court, holds a pencil in his right hand, which rests on his thigh. The upper lip on the left side of the face is swollen and shadows the cheek. A tumour.

1. Jacques-Louis David: *Self-Portrait, 1791*
2. Jacques-Louis David: *Self-Portrait, 1794*
3. Georges Rouget: *Portrait of Jacques-Louis David, c. 1815*

Francesco Salviati: *Self-Portrait, 1560*

A tumour on the right side or on the left side?

He holds a brush in his left hand; he holds a pencil in his right. Is he left-handed or right-handed or both? The left-handed David's eyes stare into a mirror, a single mirror. The right-handed David was portrayed by Georges Rouget, one of his pupils, and the master himself is said to have retouched this portrait, to make it a better likeness. To look at a portrait of David is not the same as looking at David: it is looking at him in and through a mirror.

Perverse reflection (assumption)

He looks at himself in a mirror. The finished canvas resembles the mirror. This painted face *is not* the painter's face: it is symmetrical with it. (He holds the brush in his left hand; what a lot of portraits are *left-handed* . . .) This painted equivalence is not identity.

As a result of the mirror, the self-portrait is *out-of-true*, a scandal insidious, specious and secretly condemned. The *right* hand is the hand of the oath, the hand of might; it is for dexterity; it is the basis of *rectitude* and *uprightness*. Perjury, treachery, clumsiness are attributes of the left hand, together with all that is base, suspicious, cowardly or sinister. The left is the wrong side, where gloom, disgrace and fear abound. The *right* way round brings certainty and glory. (The president of an assembly who had just been elected by a conservative majority called upon this majority to seat itself in the place of honour on his right. Order, the past, lack of mobility became the right; the will to justice the left. This late acceptation in the realm of politics dates in France from the beginnings of the Third Republic and is nothing more than a perversion of the mark of honour that this president wished to show.)

On the right praise; on the left blame.

The out-of-true equivalence that is the portrait disturbs us, as would the presence of an insistent look.

The portrait, an authentic copy of the mirror, is a mirror. I (I is the person looking at this portrait) look at myself in it. Only my presence can put to rights the painted portrait that in me finds its sense – of direction.

The portrait of the painter by himself, done with a mirror, requires the presence of a spectator. This requirement on the part of the painter is an appeal on behalf of painting itself. *Someone must be there to look at it.*

Drawing and nature

Accessories should play the same role in a picture as confidants do in tragedies.[1]

Ingres

Jean-Dominique Ingres is twenty-four years old. Standing in his studio, the painter is at his easel. Behind him a neutral-coloured wall is bare. A thick, heavy coat seems to weigh down his shoulders and hangs practically without any folds. The painter's right fist grasps a stick of white chalk which conceals the thickness of the thumb. In his left hand, the arm almost fully stretched out, he holds a crumpled rag. And this gesture is practically similar to that of Salviati in his self-portrait, with a rag in his closed right fist – the portrait was for the collection of the Grand Dukes of Tuscany – and the rag is being used to wipe out a sketch for a portrait. What uncertain, indecisive detail is Ingres wiping away? What error is he putting right? The model, Jean-François Gilibert, who is no doubt present, is posing motionless. The painter is watching him. In a moment he will turn away from him, from this model who is on his right and is holding the pose, and will start drawing on the canvas covered with fine dust from the wiped-out chalk, and then, with a serious mien, he will turn back again towards the model. And the same gestures will be repeated for hours.

With the crumpled rag in his left hand he wipes away the uncertainties and doubts of a sketch where we see the last remains of the outline drawing.

Jean-Dominique Ingres is drawing. He isn't painting. In front of him the palette hangs on the easel. It is too soon for it to be of any use.

Photograph by Charles Marville showing the first state of Ingres'
Self-Portrait at the Age of Twenty-Four

Jean-Auguste-Dominique Ingres:
Self-Portrait at the Age of Twenty-Four, 1804, reworked in 1850

The self-portrait is a confession. Ingres kept drawing: jottings and sketches disprove or confirm each other, resuming, correcting, defining or cancelling out. "What takes longest is conceiving one's picture as a whole."[2] It is this period of doubts gradually resolved by sketch after sketch that constitutes the self-portrait's confession. Certainty arises out of doubt resolved. Ingres starts by effacing the picture he is about to paint. "Draw a long time before you think of painting"[2]: this will be Ingres' advice to his students. We have to imagine him, an old man in Paris, practically in tears: "Ah, my friend, it's very bad, I can no longer draw. I know nothing any more. A woman's portrait! The most difficult thing in the world, quite out of the question... I'm going to have another try tomorrow, because I'm starting from scratch again... really, I could burst into tears."[1]

The self-portrait is a lie. The shadow of the chin on the painter's neck and the shadow of the outstretched arm on the canvas move towards the wall. The painter is thus facing the studio window or glass front, the direction from which the light comes; judging by the angle of the shadows, at that hour the sun is high. The model Jean-Dominique Ingres is looking at turns his back to this window. We have to imagine his face against the light, his features are indistinct and heavily shadowed. So it isn't this model Jean-Dominique Ingres is looking at, but rather his own face with the light falling on it from in front, his double in the mirror. Jean-François Gilibert is not posing, and this portrait of Jean-Dominique Ingres by himself remains in Ingres' studio. In 1850, Jean-François Gilibert dies.

Ingres returns to his portrait painted nearly fifty years earlier and puts an end to the painted incoherence that presupposes the presence of the model. (Is it this death of a friend that makes it possible for the canvas to be reworked? Is the portrait sketch of Gilibert that disappeared under the over-painting the death of a friendship recounted? Is this gesture that of forgetting?) "Art never achieves so high a degree of perfection as when it resembles nature so strongly that one can take it for nature itself."[2]

The corrections have been made: the left hand, bright against the shadow of the head on the wall, rests open on the shirt; there is a ring on the middle finger and a part of the other fingers is hidden by the box-coat worn open. The picture that was once there is now invisible and all that can be seen is a piece of chassis with nails in it to stretch the canvas: this portrait is now only the portrait of the painter by himself. He has submitted "to nature."

It will have taken Ingres fifty years to paint this self-portrait, which first proclaims the primacy of drawing, and then, after being corrected, tells us that nature and nature alone should be the model.

First digression concerning the mirrors painted by Ingres

Madame de Senonnes (1814-1816), Madame Moitessier (1852-1856), both seated, and the Countess d'Haussonville (1845) standing, leaning against a mantelpiece, turn their backs to a mirror. The reflection shows their bare necks and their different chignons; fashion has changed in forty years.

I examine these mirrors. What causes the right temple under the pulled-back hair traversing Madame de Senonnes' right ear to be lighted up in this dull mirror? This temple is in the shadows and the hair does not have the reflected light that the mirror shows. How is it that the Countess d'Hauss-onville's index finger under her chin can be seen in the mirror in a line with the red ribbon in her hair, whereas the shadow of the finger on the neck indicates that this index finger is in front of the neck itself? How does it come about that Madame Moitessier's profile is painted in the mirror, whereas seated as she is in front of it in a red armchair, she is turning her back to it, which is rather evident from the horizontal section of the frame?

A light on a temple, an index finger, a profile, these are all impossible reflections. There is something odd about the mirrors that Ingres used.

Jean-Auguste-Dominique Ingres: ▷
The Comtesse d'Haussonville, 1845

Jean-Auguste-Dominique Ingres:
The Vicomtesse de Senonnes, 1814-1816

Jean-Auguste-Dominique Ingres:
Madame Moitessier, 1852-1856

Jean-Auguste-Dominique Ingres:
Portrait of Poussin (from The Apotheosis of Homer, 1827)

Nicolas Poussin: *Self-Portrait, 1650*

**Second digression
in which Poussin's self-portrait
as copied and modified
acts as a manifesto**

> *I think I'll manage to be original
> by imitating others.*[1]
>
> Ingres

For the catalogue of paintings of the Charles X Museum, a catalogue that never appeared, Ingres wrote the following commentary on his *Apotheosis of Homer*: "Near the bottom of the picture, shown as half-figures, are Tasso, Shakespeare, Corneille, La Fontaine, Mozart and Poussin; the latter holding a portfolio containing his studies, points to the Ancients with a grave and confident gesture as the only models worth following."[2]

Ingres copied the self-portrait that Poussin painted in 1650 for Chantelou (as he copied Raphael's around 1820-1824). The copy is an exact one: the folds of the black cloak, almost a toga, worn by the painter, are the same, the red knot of the ribbon holding the portfolio shut is the same, perpendicular to the ring on the little finger of Poussin's right hand. Poussin's "grave and confident gesture" (Poussin who wrote to Cassiano del Pozzo on the 4th of April 1642: "I am a good innovator"[3]), in which he has his left arm raised with the finger pointing at Apelles, is an invention of Ingres. Apelles, a young man wearing a blue toga, is followed by Raphael, whose hand he holds. Beside them, Virgil and Dante guided by him.

A genealogical descent is created by this copy of Poussin's self-portrait: Apelles, Raphael, Poussin, Ingres. This loyalty to the revered masters of the past is a manifesto of Ingres' artistic ideals.

A further proof of this genealogical creation: when Dürer learned that, according to Pliny, Apelles used the imperfect tense,[4] he started signing his finished works with the mention *"faciebat"* and no longer *"fecit."* *The Apotheosis of Homer* has the signature at the bottom left, INGRES PING^{BAT}, and at the bottom right the date, ANNO 1827. Ingres too followed Apelles by using the imperfect tense, i.e. *"pingebat"* and not *"pinxit."*

The first canvas on which Ingres used the imperfect tense was *Oedipus and the Sphinx*, which bears the inscription: I. INGRES PINGEBAT 1808.

Oedipus, the Sphinx, Apelles, Ingres. The thread of meaning is complete.

Jean-Auguste-Dominique Ingres: *The Apotheosis of Homer, 1827*

Jan Frans Douven: *Self-Portrait with the Portrait of the Elector
Johann Wilhelm von der Pfalz and his Wife Anna Maria Louise, c. 1693*

Katharina van Hemessen: *Self-Portrait at the Easel, 1548*

Understatement

The canvas seen from the back, with the cross-pieces of the frame visible, was the portrait of Philip IV of Spain with Queen Mariana; Velázquez was painting. And Goya painted Charles IV surrounded by his family. Douven points at the portrait of the Elector Johann Wilhelm von der Pfalz, seen in profile with his wife Anna Maria Louise. The same portrait of this Elector crowned with glory as a reward for being a patron of the arts dominates the self-portrait of Adriaen van der Werff, held by a muse or a nymph whose breast is uncovered. Katharina van Hemessen appears to have done a portrait of Queen Mary of Hungary in 1548; it is a framed sketch on an easel. She was later to accompany the queen to the court of Spain. The sketched-out face on the canvas painted by Elisabeth Vigée-Lebrun is that of Marie-Antoinette, Queen of France. Still unfinished, the portrait of Gustav III of Sweden faces Alexander Roslin.

The painter portrays himself as the painter of his sovereign, patron and protector.

Only Goya, towards the rear behind the royal family group, is present with the King in the same space. It is only a mirror reflection that informs us that Philip IV is present in front of Velázquez; Philip IV does not form part of the area shown in

paint. Katharina van Hemessen, Alexander Roslin, and Elisabeth Vigée-Lebrun are painting: is it the royal model that they are looking at or are they working in his absence? The very absence of these crowned heads is understatement. The reigning monarch is the model and never ceases to be the model.

If the portrait of the painter by himself is the response to the question "Who am I?" or to the command "Know thyself!", for a long time the only reply was: "I am king's painter." Here, instead of the self-portrait as confession, we have the self-portrait as affirmation of a title and position. But Louis XIV is Apollo, the Medici are the Magi Kings and Napoleon is Caesar: the substantial power of myths and echoes inspires make-believe.

Delacroix may paint *Liberty Guiding the People*. Some commentators state that the bearded young man wearing a top hat, a young bourgeois of the national guard armed with a hunting rifle, is Delacroix himself. What is Liberty ordering?

Louis-Philippe's umbrella inspires no make-believe; and neither does Guizot's order "Get rich!", which the Second Empire obeys. Interests or pensions cannot be painted. Profit is not an accomplice of make-believe.

What remains is reality; what remains is solitude. What remains is painting.

Elisabeth Vigée-Lebrun: *Self-Portrait at the Easel, c. 1791*

1. Théodore Géricault: *Portrait of an Artist in his Studio,
   1818*
2. Tommaso Minardi: *Self-Portrait in his Attic Room, 1813?*

fist. He is day-dreaming. The shadow hollows out his cheeks and his lips are set in a disillusioned smile. The skull laughs, the plaster model groans; the face of this young man, solitary between laughter and groaning, loses itself in its sad musing.

Another attic room. The ceiling slopes down towards a low window of which the inner shutter is open, and daylight shows the disorder of want: books and sheets of paper are crammed into the shelves of a narrow book-case; the bed is unmade and its sheets crumpled; a table is overloaded with papers, files, books and a straw-bottomed chair. No doubt this room has another window which directly illuminates the young man seated on a mattress placed on the floor on a straw mattress which serves as a bedstead; a sheet of paper and a pair of compasses are lying about on the grey and white striped mattress cloth. On the floor there is what may be an ox's skull and on a crate, level with the young man's shoulder covered with a blanket, a skull.

The young man, dressed in dark clothing and wrapped in a black cape, sits unevenly on this mattress on the floor, his face impassive and weary. Maybe, just a moment ago, he was contemplating the skull facing him with its hollow eye-sockets, and he was in a reverie. Maybe, in a minute, he will again pick up the sheet of paper lying within arm's reach on the bed and continue the work he had dropped. Maybe...

Solitude and hard times

*Artists: Praise their
disinterestedness (old).*[1]
Flaubert

An attic room; the rafters stick into the wall covered by irregularly rough-cast plaster. We must imagine that under this roof the heat will be like a furnace in the summer and in winter the cold will chill to the marrow. On an unpainted wooden shelf are a skull and a grinning plaster head placed side by side. A palette hangs on the wall. In front of this lack-lustre wall a young man is seated, pensive, on a straw-bottomed chair. (For a long time this portrait was said to be a portrait of Géricault by himself, but the assumption was rejected. This portrait is nothing other than the portrait of a young man to whom one person or another attributes one name or another among the painter's friends; and these are other assumptions.) The young man, in evening dress, wearing a tie, is alone, leaning against the chair-back on his elbow and resting his head on his

likely there is still a little heat left in this fireplace which will only just be enough to reheat the soup and the coffee. A young man is sitting there, leaning against a vertical mount of the fireplace with his legs stretched out; a cat, also come to warm itself, sits there too. The young man – we can see from his face that he is close to tears – is peeling the potatoes set down beside him in a cloth. Being a painter also means this: a potato in a box of paints, a squashed tube with the paint running out onto the floor, a neglected easel; being a painter is also never being able to be anything more than a dauber. Everyone has been a dauber, in the sense that this has meant joining the studio at an early age and starting to learn to paint. But being a dauber, a bad painter,

Standing before a narrow unmade bed, the sheets grey in the shadow, is a young man. He is naked to the waist, with his shirt all creased, stuffed into his belt and falling down over his hips. The young man is painting; the young man is painting himself. The mirror in which he looks at himself makes him left-handed and so he paints himself left-handed, with his left hand holding a piece of chalk between finger and thumb resting on the canvas. His right hand, palm downwards, lies loosely on his hip among the folds of his shirt. The young man is painting himself; he is painting weariness; his torso has hollows as do his ribs; a shoulder droops. On the table on his right is an open box of paints and a few flowers which are already fading. These fading flowers are, as a skull would be, another Vanitas element.

Vanity, vanity, all is vanity . . .

The box of paints open on the floor, neglected, like the easel leaning against the mantelpiece, on which stand a lamp, a book, a jug, a coffee pot, as well as a piece of bread, stale no doubt; behind them is a mirror. Another coffee pot stands in the fireplace itself beside a sort of soup tureen. Most

equally means reaching the age when you have lost all your illusions which vanish when your hopes are disappointed, and you know that all you can be sure of is failure and disappointment and gradually becoming "as poor as a painter," as an expression of the time had it.

There remains "that inexpressible something that people call hard times. A horrible state in which there are days without bread, nights without sleep, evenings without a candle, weeks without work, the future without hope, the hole in the elbow of your coat, your old hat that makes the young girls laugh, the door you find locked against you at night because you haven't paid your rent, the porter's insolence and the jeers of your cheap restaurant owner, your neighbours' sniggers, all the humiliations, dignity trampled on, any sort of work accepted, the disgust, the bitterness, the feeling of being weighted down."[2] A tube of paint: tubes, first made of copper, then of tin, replaced the bladders in 1824. They sold for something like twenty-five centimes to a franc and there were certain rare reds costing as much as ten or fifteen francs a tube. For the price of a tube of paint one could eat three meals a day, three square meals: breakfast, dinner and supper. An easel could run to one hundred francs, and the mixing pans, maulstick, and brushes two or three times more. A painter needed a minimum of 150 to 200 francs a month to live on. In 1841 Ingres was paid 100,000 francs for the ceiling of the Throne Room of the Chambre des Pairs. Then Madame Ingres could give up her dress-making. But there is only one Chambre des Pairs and only one Throne Room in the Chambre des Pairs. During the last years of his life, Delacroix received a pension of 10,000 francs; and Van Gogh lived on the 150 francs a month sent him by his brother Theo, who worked for Goupil, a paint and picture dealer with branches in London, Brussels, The Hague, Berlin and New York as well as two galleries in Paris, all of this as early as the Second Empire. And speculation in paintings changed nothing of the painter's lot. Millet's *Angelus* actually fetched 553,000 francs at the Secretan sale in 1889, a price never attained by a painting until then. In 1860 Millet had sold this same *Angelus* for 1,000 francs, already a good price. Between 1862 and 1866 Manet sold nothing. As for Monet, in 1877 he sold his pictures for forty, sometimes fifty francs.[3]

Artists: "all wild young fellows, they earn a mint of money, but throw it all out of the window."[1]

It was this dual solitude, meditative and disillusioned, that was created by Romanticism, and the solitude of destitution was that painted by Géricault, Minardi, Janssen and Tassaert. Another name for this dual solitude is Bohemia.

The story behind the portrait

"During my life I've done masses of portraits of myself that reflect changes in my state of mind; I've written my life, in a word."[1] So says Courbet. What life-story do we find in these portraits?

1842: *A Small Portrait of the Artist with a Black Dog.* Gustave Courbet is twenty-three. He is seated behind a table or a balustrade on which his hand rests; a black spaniel cocks its head in front of his chest, its front paws presumably in the young man's lap. Long hair frames his face, emphasized by the whiteness of the shirt collar which, like the sleeve, emerges from a black jacket, a sort of doublet. Does this austerity stem from the Great Century of Louis XIV, or is it part of Romanticism?

At twenty-three Gustave Courbet is austere, adopting the posture of Parmigianino distorted by the convex mirror, with a spaniel in his lap.

The Portrait of the Artist or The Desperate Man is signed and dated: "41 G. Courbet." This is an improbable date. Should it be 1841 or 1843? Courbet is twenty-two or twenty-three. And, wild-looking, he stares straight at you. What dreadful horror that has seized his inner being is he fleeing in terror? His shoulders are held forward at an angle. His hands grasp at his hair to pull it back, but a lock falls loose. He seems to be falling or running. Fear, flight, dizziness; the flight and the falling are found again in *Mad With Fear*. His lips are closed. No cry will assuage this despair. Could this painted terror be no more than a studio exercise, a sort of defence and illustration of the *Lecture on the Expression of the Passions* that Le Brun gave at the Academy in 1668? Or

Gustave Courbet:

1. *Small Portrait of the Artist with a Black Dog, 1842*
2. *Portrait of the Artist or The Desperate Man, 1843?*
3. *Mad with Fear or The Desperate Man, c. 1844-1845*
4. *Portrait of the Artist or Courbet with a Black Dog, c. 1844*

again, Lavater's *Fragments of Physiognomy*, published between 1775 and 1778? These assumptions are less than certain, and if the terror really is an "illustration" of this kind, there is a reason for Courbet's choice of it. The portrait tells us nothing of the reasons for the despair.

1842 or 1844? *Portrait of the Artist or Courbet with a Black Dog.* This portrait was hung in the Salon of 1844. This was the first time that Courbet himself exhibited at the Salon. The arrangement of the hair is unchanged; the black spaniel is the same; the same illuminated white collar emphasizes the face. Courbet out for a walk; his stick and his book are on the ground behind him, and he is seated in a landscape. (This is not the first portrait in which he paints himself in a landscape: he painted himself sitting under a tree at the age of fourteen.) Who is this young man smoking a pipe that he holds in his right hand at rest on his knee? A painter? The only confirmation is to be found in the title: "Portrait of the Artist." Jacob More, for example, among others, also painted himself in a landscape. We may ask if what Courbet is saying here is intended to be the counterpart of the English neo-classical landscape painters, or of romantic painters throughout all Europe, seen in solitary state in a landscape.

Gustave Courbet: *The Sculptor, 1844-1845*

Gustave Courbet: *The Draughts Players, 1844*

1844 again: *The Draughts Players*. Gustave Courbet, self-portrayed on the right, wears similar clothes, a sort of disguise; his chin is prolonged by a sharp pointed little beard. Framed pictures hang on the wall; an anatomical plaster model said to represent Michelangelo stands on a bookcase in front of a jar crammed with paint brushes. A row of pipes hang from a rack on the wall behind the sort of cap Courbet is wearing. A romantic spree.

1844 or 1845? *The Sculptor*. Dressed in the clothes of another age which belong to the make-believe of the time, a young man is seated smiling and leaning his head on his shoulder; doubtless he is day-dreaming. In his right hand a mallet, in his left a chisel. Presumably, in a brief moment when he has had his rest he will start work again on the sculpture of the young woman leaning on an amphora that he is cutting directly in the rock. Is it this young man's wish to be an apprentice Freemason? The woman-fountain, the mallet, and the chisel are no doubt symbols of Freemasonry. Courbet, still beardless, is perhaps claiming to be a Freemason. Does he yet belong to a Lodge?

1844: *The Lovers in the Country, Youthful Feelings, Paris*. Their profiles are turned in the same direction, but the young woman's face leans towards her right shoulder and Courbet's face, framed by a narrow beard, towards his left. Courbet's hand holds the woman's in his and their thumbs cross. They are waltzing. Courbet in love is dancing.

Gustave Courbet: *The Lovers in the Country,*
Youthful Feelings, Paris, 1844

Gustave Courbet:
Portrait of the Artist
or The Man with a Leather Belt,
c. 1845-1846

1845, perhaps 1846: *Portrait of the Artist or The Man with a Leather Belt.* We see a pensive young man, his upper lip and chin show the moustache and beard he is growing. His chin rests on the back and fingers of his right hand; his elbow leans on a portfolio with a pencil on it. A plaster model is to be seen on the table behind the painter's shoulder. The thumb of his left hand is hooked behind the buckle of his wide leather belt. Is this portrait the portrait of the dreamy assurance of someone who, having spent a great deal of time in the Louvre copying the Old Masters, is starting to become Courbet? (Immediately below this man with the belt by Courbet is Titian's *Man with a Glove.*)

1847: *The Cellist, Portrait of the Artist*. This cellist is left-handed. In 1847 Gustave Courbet paints himself as a cellist . . . which means?

1849? *Portrait of the Artist or The Man with a Pipe*. "It's the portrait of a fanatic, of an aesthete, it's the portrait of a man who has been disillusioned by the stupidities that have been part of his education and who is trying to settle down on principles of his own," wrote Courbet to Alfred Bruyas, of Montpellier, who purchased the portrait. A fanatic? An aesthete? Disillusioned? We ask about this bearded young man with the dishevelled hair who is smoking his pipe. The portrait itself says nothing of fanaticism. The pouting lips, the heaviness of the eyelids, are they supposed to show disillusionment? Perhaps. Nearly thirty years old, Courbet is smoking a pipe. This is the only certainty stated by the portrait. Is this a man trying to "settle down on principles of his own"?

1853? *Portrait of the Artist by Himself*. A bust. Almost full-face, bearded, the hair lightly dishevelled.

1853? *Portrait of the Artist by Himself*. A bust, three-quarter angle. The same beard, hair cut short.

Gustave Courbet:

1. *The Cellist, Portrait of the Artist, 1847*

2. *Portrait of the Artist or The Man with a Pipe, 1849?*

3. *Portrait of the Artist by Himself, 1853?*

4. *Portrait of the Artist by Himself, 1853?*

111

Gustave Courbet:

1. *Portrait of the Artist or The Wounded Man, 1844, repainted in 1854*

2. *X-ray photograph of Courbet's Wounded Man*

3. *The Meeting or Bonjour Monsieur Courbet, 1854*

4. *Portrait of the Artist or Courbet with a Striped Collar, 1854*

5. *Self-portrait drawing, head study for The Painter's Studio*

6. *Self-Portrait, detail of The Painter's Studio, 1855*

1854: *Portrait of the Artist or The Wounded Man.*
Les parfums ne font pas frissonner sa narine;
Il dort dans le soleil, la main sur la poitrine
Tranquille. Il a deux trous rouges au côté droit.[2]

(The *description* is by Rimbaud.) He appears to be
sleeping; his shirt is stained with blood; his hand on
his stomach grips a fold of his coat. Anybody looking at this wounded man in 1854 only sees a wounded man. A duel, perhaps, for there is a sword on
the tree-trunk against which the man is resting. But
the wound is something else entirely: this man
about to die is part of a repainted canvas: in 1844,
lying next to a young woman, their arms round
each other, he was resting with her at the foot of this
tree. The lovers in the country had dozed off. Alone
and mortally wounded, ten years later, Courbet is
about to die. The tenderness of the siesta has been
effaced and a wounded man remains. But the repainting hides the metaphor itself.

1854: *The Meeting or Bonjour Monsieur Courbet.*
A road. In the distance a coach is driving away.
Courbet is being greeted by Alfred Bruyas, followed
by his servant Calas, and accompanied by his dog,
Breton. These gentlemen have removed their hats,
but only Bruyas, and his bowing servant, are actually in the act of greeting. (Courbet, when he is
greeting, doesn't say what he is greeting, or else he
chooses to greet the sea.) Courbet stands up straight
again. Bruyas' wealth greets Courbet's talent.
Bruyas lives in Montpellier; this meeting then takes
place in the countryside not far from the town. This
portrait only specifies one thing more: without a
doubt Courbet paints out of doors; on his back he
carries an easel and a painting box.

1854: *Portrait of the Artist or Courbet with a Striped
Collar.* Courbet bearded, short-haired, in profile.
Nothing else, except the striped collar which labels
the portrait itself.

A sheet of tracing paper. On it Courbet has
copied the portrait with a striped collar. In the centre of *The Studio*, in 1855, his self-portrait will be the
same: his jacket collar will be similarly striped.

113

Gustave Courbet: *Portrait of the Artist at Sainte-Pélagie, 1873-1874?*

False, *since Realism does exist . . .*[4] Compromised by his adherence to the Paris Commune (March-May 1871) and charged with responsibility for the destruction of the Vendôme column, Courbet was imprisoned at Sainte-Pélagie. The red foulard that he wears knotted like a cravat round his neck may be an allusion to the left-wing extremism of the Commune.

1875? 1876? *Self-Portrait*.
The thickened face is seen in profile. Courbet is heavy and thick. Courbet, embittered, is in exile. The portrait says nothing of the bitterness, it is silent about the exile.

1840 to 1875. A span of thirty-five years. What narrative content do Courbet's self-portraits have. What is Courbet trying to *tell* us?

Gustave Courbet: *Self-Portrait, 1875-1876?*

Twenty years pass.
1873? 1874? *Portrait of the Artist at Sainte-Pélagie*. Courbet in prison, wearing a beret and smoking a pipe, sitting on the sill of an open window. Behind the window are bars; it overlooks a courtyard with trees.

> *Dans Sainte-Pélagie*
> *Sous ce règne élargie,*
> *Où rêveur et pensif,*
>   *Je vis captif,*
>
> *Pas une herbe ne pousse*
> *Et pas un brin de mousse*
> *Le long des murs grillés*
>   *Et frais taillés.*[3]

This *commentary* is by Gérard de Nerval. The "not a blade of grass" is just as false as the black beard and the disillusioned and sly smile of the other.

Philippe de Champaigne: *Self-Portrait, 1668.*
Replica by the artist's nephew Jean-Baptiste de Champaigne

ted to do it, saying that I was too small to be lodged in the company of his great men.)

For his family Philippe de Champaigne agreed to paint himself. Naturalized French in 1629, in 1668 behind his portrait he painted his native city of Brussels.

On the orders of the Grand Duke of Tuscany, Antoine de Favray, born at Bagnolet in the eastern suburbs of Paris, painted himself as an oriental philosopher decorated with the Order of the Knights of Malta, with as a background, Constantinople, where he spent ten years of his life.

Champaigne was sixty-six years old, Favray seventy-two, and their portraits are memoirs.

Antoine de Favray: *Self-Portrait, 1778*

St. Gudula and St. Sophia

Philippe de Champaigne in the act of turning, his torso in profile, his right hand held against his chest. In his left hand he holds a scroll on which the date of the portrait is written: 1668. Behind him a tree-trunk wreathed in ivy. In the background a landscape with towers and a spire. Philippe de Champaigne is standing on the edge of the Cambre forest. The spire is that of St. Michael's, and the towers those of St. Gudula's. There, in Brussels, he had been baptised on the 2nd of May 1602.

Antoine de Favray is posing; his left hand is most likely on the sill of a window indicated by the curtain behind him. "I portrayed myself as an oriental philosopher."[1] He is wearing a fur hat, and his coat trimmed with the same fur is worn open. Malta was to be the scene of his death in 1792 when he was "Comandante di Valcanville" in the Order of Knights. Behind him can be seen the minarets and cupolas of St. Sophia. Favray spent nearly ten years in Constantinople, from 1762 to 1771. After Bettino de Ricci, in charge at the time of collecting self-portraits of painters, had written numerous letters in vain, the Grand Duke of Tuscany had to issue an order to obtain Favray's consent to paint himself. *"Non l'ho mai voluto fare, dicendo che ero troppo piccolo per essere allogiato con suoi grandi uomini."*[1] (I never wan-

Hans Holbein the Younger: *Self-Portrait
at the Age of Forty-Five, 1542-1543*

... Et in secula seculorum

ALBERTUS DURERUS NORICUS...
IOANNES HOLPENIUS BASILEENSIS...
EFFIGIES NICOLAI POVSSINI ANDELYENSIS...
J.A.D. INGRES Pictor Gallicus...

Dürer, Holbein, Poussin and Ingres signed their
portraits of themselves. Their names and their or-
igins are stated in this tongue which, in their day,
would assure them of being read and understood by
all Europe. And this language is the one in which
we read in Pliny that Apelles used the imperfect
tense; and *"faciebat"* and *"pingebat"* replaced *"fecit"*
and *"pinxit."* And this language, because it is the
language of the Church, assured them that once
read, they would be understood by the centuries,
and in the centuries of centuries.

In the portrait of the painter by himself, from
Apelles in the imperfect tense to the coming centuries appealed to by Apelles and his compeers, lies
eternity.

Orders and decorations

*I am relying a great deal on my
old age; it will avenge me.*[1]

Ingres

"On his buttoned coat he was wearing his badge
of grand officer of the Order and beneath his white
cravat one could see the black, silver-edged ribbon
with the Prussian cross of merit which he had been
awarded. One scarcely dared to speak to him, so
severe was his aspect and so imposing the prestige of
his name."[2]

Ingres wore the same decorations for the self-
portrait he painted in 1859, the lapel of the coat half
hidden, the red and white white ribbon and the medal
surmounted by the Grand Ducal Crown of the
Order of Merit of St. Joseph of Tuscany, showing
bright in the shadow of the top hat held in the left
hand in its butter coloured glove. Ingres had received this Tuscan decoration one year previously.
On the 30th of May 1858 he wrote to Marcotte:
"Our friend Gatteaux [does he mean Nicolas-
Marie or Edouard? Both were engravers of medals,
and Edouard was a resident student at the French
Academy in Rome], who at the moment is in
Florence, is a witness of all the honourable feelings
that are being expressed about this portrait, which,
unpretentious though it is, it may well lay claim to.
The Grand Duke has had him as a guest for some
time in the Pitti Palace. And lastly, having judged
it worthy to be hung beside the portraits of the great
painters in the Uffizi Gallery, the portrait is to be
placed there and its author decorated with the
Order of Merit of St. Joseph of Tuscany."[3]

Ingres' self-assurance was now beyond question.
In February 1854 the Emperor Napoleon III did
him the honour of visiting him[4] in a studio lent by
Gatteaux for the occasion, and on the 15th of
November 1855, Napoleon III himself made Ingres
a Grand Officer in the Order of the Legion of Honour. The lapel of the coat turned down over the
badge, hides its centre, featuring the emblem of the
Empire, the Imperial Eagle encircled by the words
engraved in roman letters HONNEUR ET PATRIE. This
is not to be taken as a token of political prudence.
Ingres was faithful to the Empire; the *coup d'Etat* of
the 2nd of December 1851 was to his satisfaction.
Ingres never ceased to be faithful. He was made
Chevalier of the Legion of Honour under Charles X
in 1825, and in 1833 and 1845, under the July
Monarchy, Officer, then Commander. On the 24th
of February 1848, with revolution breaking out in
Paris, Flandrin chanced to meet Ingres on the Quai
Voltaire: he was rushing to the Tuileries to defend
Louis-Philippe. Ingres became a "Regency man."[4]
Ingres was faithful to the established power. Ingres
never ceased to be faithful to it.

Jean-Auguste-Dominique Ingres: *Self-Portrait at the Age of Seventy-Nine, 1859*

"There is more of an analogy than one might think between good taste and good morals," proclaimed Ingres. (Doubtless he was bristling and hurt because when the picture committee was set up for the Paris World's Fair of 1855, both he and Delacroix were on it: "I am of the same rank as the apostle of ugliness!")[1]

The case against good taste was summed up by a French poet:

> Le bon goût, c'est une grille,
> Gare à ce vieux bon goût-là!
> De tout temps sous son étrille,
> Pan, le bouc sacré, bêla!
>
> Le goût classe, isole, trie,
> Et de crainte des ébats,
> Met de la serrurerie
> Autour de tout, ici-bas.
>
> Il cloître, et dit j'émancipe.
> Il coupe, et dit j'ai créé.
> Etre sobre est son principe,
> Des malades agréé.
>
> Il est cousin de l'envie,
> Il est membre des sénats.
> Il donne au cœur, à la vie,
> La forme d'un cadenas.[5]

That poet was Victor Hugo, who went into exile under the Second Empire (1852-1870).

Ingres, staying home, chose good taste, good morals and the Empire. Good taste, says Hugo, is a "member of the Senates." On the 25th of May 1862 Ingres was appointed a Senator.

On the self-portrait which he sent to the Grand Duke of Tuscany in 1858, he wrote: J.A.D. INGRES Pictor Gallicus SE IPSUM Pxt Anno Aetatis LXXVIII MDCCCLVIII. Pictor Gallicus, French painter: so he described himself and that was enough. In 1854 he had portrayed himself in the painting he made of *Joan of Arc at the Coronation of King Charles VII in Rheims Cathedral*: standing back, his hands crossed on the pommel of his sword, he is Joan's armour bearer, Doloy. Still faithful.

The 1859 portrait of Ingres by himself, a variant of the one he sent the previous year to Florence, is the pendant of the one he painted of his second wife, "née Ramel," as we read in the inscription painted high up on the right. He married her on the 15th of April 1852. Almost forty years earlier, on the 4th of December 1813, he had married Madeleine Chapelle at San Martino dei Monti in Rome. "Madame Ingres was sent out to me from France. And she didn't know me either . . . that's to say, I had sent her a little sketch I had made of myself."

"And you even flattered yourself quite a bit," said Madame Ingres without putting down her knitting.[6]

1. Jean-Auguste-Dominique Ingres: *Joan of Arc at the Coronation of King Charles VII in Rheims Cathedral (detail), 1854*

2. Jean-Auguste-Dominique Ingres: *Self-Portrait at the Age of Seventy-Eight, 1858*

Eugène Delacroix: *Self-Portrait, c. 1842*

the bequest of one's self-portrait? Is this portrait the expression of this solitude? "They have painted their souls in painting things, and your own soul is also asking for its turn. And why revolt against one's order?"[3] Is it his very soul that he is giving away?

Is the portrait of Delacroix by himself the evidence of the "inevitable solitude" of a heart or the reply to the order of a soul? This question and this alternative find only the echo of silence in the portraits themselves. The diary and only the diary can ask the question and ask it in this particular manner.

Was the Louvre portrait of Delacroix by himself (dated here to c. 1839) actually painted in 1834, as some think? Or in 1837, or between 1838 and 1840? What does the actual date matter? The one point to note is that this self-portrait of Delacroix was painted during the period when his diary was silent, broken off from 1824 to 1847. Silence of Delacroix's diary: self-portrait of Delacroix.

Which model?

The things you experience when you are alone are far stronger and fresher.[1]

Delacroix

"I bequeath to Monsieur Blondel, Counsellor of State, my portrait, which is not quite finished. The background is very dark, the coat black. I keenly regret that I am not in a position to give him another token of my deeply felt friendship," wrote Delacroix on the 3rd of August 1863 in his Will.

Forty years earlier, he noted in his diary: "Too often you reproach yourself for having changed, but it's things that have changed. What can be more disheartening? I've two, three or four friends: well, I'm obliged to be a different man with each of them, or rather, to show each of them the face he understands. It's one of the greatest sources of unhappiness never to be able to be fully known and understood by one single man; and when I think about it, I believe it is life's most hurtful wound; it is this inevitable solitude to which our hearts are condemned."[2]

Who was Delacroix, who knew himself to be condemned to solitude even in his friendship for his friend Monsieur Blondel? What sort of bequest is

Eugène Delacroix: *Self-Portrait, c. 1839*

The fact that this portrait of Delacroix was painted during the years when his diary was silent does not prove that it replaced the diary. Memoirs, a diary or confessions are accounts of facts; a portrait is a fact.

Rembrandt's self-portraits are not the story of Rembrandt's life and are not his diary. From the self-portrait of 1626 to that of 1669, no story is being written. The wrinkles which from portrait to portrait are carved deeper and deeper into Rembrandt's face tell us about time. These portraits tell us nothing about the story of Rembrandt's life. The portraits are not portraits of Rembrandt as a *widower* or Rembrandt *in his downfall*; they are just portraits of Rembrandt and the wrinkles that vex and incise his features are no more than a description of years lived. The series of portraits of Rembrandt is not a diary.

The piece of paper held by Giorgione's old woman in the Accademia Museum in Venice, with the words COL TEMPO written on it, is reminiscent of the series of Rembrandt portraits. With time... With each portrait Rembrandt catches time red-handed, catches it in the act.

4

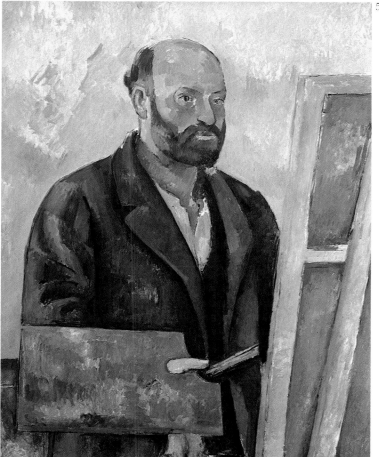

5

The Louvre portrait of Delacroix of c. 1839 is not a continuation of his diary, as the portraits of Rembrandt are neither the story, the confessions nor the diary of his life.

They are portraits.

"I paint a head as I paint a door, or anything else,"[4] proclaims Cézanne.

Giacometti comments: "In painting the left ear, in establishing more of a correlation between the left ear and the background than with the right ear, more of a correlation between the colour of the hair and the colour of the cranium, Cézanne has eliminated – and yet what it was he wanted, was really to achieve a complete head – he has totally eliminated the concept we had before him of the unity of a head."[5]

At the time when photography was invented, the painter began ridding himself of any concern for the model and was in future solely concerned with painting itself. Until then, the portrait of the painter by himself was first and foremost a portrait *of* the painter; the model was of more importance than painting. And henceforth the primary importance is no longer the same: the portrait of the painter is first of all a portrait *by* himself. The concern is no longer the painter but his painting.

Dürer can proclaim in the imperfect tense, in the manner of Apelles, that he "was making" one portrait or another of himself. Dürer is speaking of Painting. Mondrian signs his self-portrait with a name that is no longer his. All Mondrian is talking about is *his* painting.

There is no portrait without a model. But there have been changes in the model.

Ingres' portraits of himself as an old man are in the nature of archival records. They belong to the Second Empire, and only to the Second Empire. They are portraits of Apelles in a frock coat, as a Grand Officer of the Legion of Honour. And it is not of some disaster like Sedan that Napoleon III is dreaming when he visits Ingres in his studio; like Alexander the Great who went to watch Apelles painting; like the Emperor Charles V who picked up Titian's brush when it fell to the floor. More probably Napoleon III is thinking about some distant river like the Indus, about extending the frontiers of his Empire. Thirty years go by. The Second Empire had disappeared. The Third Republic had taken its place. But Van Gogh's self-portraits do not belong to the Third Republic: they are something else.

Martyrdom

Michelangelo

James Ensor:
*Ecce Homo or Christ
and the Critics, 1891*

Michelangelo:
*Self-Portrait on the
flayed skin of St.
Bartholomew, detail of
The Last Judgment
in the Sistine Chapel,
1534-1541*

Self-portrayed as Christ scorned, flouted, lashed, crowned with thorns and held in a noose, James Ensor is flanked by two art critics, Fétis and Sulzberger, both in evening dress. Stern, merciless, sour-faced, they are his tormentors. For Ensor it was another Calvary.

This artist's martyrdom was not the first.

A flayed skin, a man's miserable remains hanging limply from the fist of St. Bartholomew. On it is painted the face of Michelangelo as St. Bartholomew tortured to death. The figure holding the skin is said to represent Aretino, another tormentor.

Michelangelo on a flayed skin. Ensor led to Calvary. Aretino, Fétis and Sulzberger as their tormentors. Painting is martyrdom.

Michelangelo tortured by Aretino (presumably it was by Aretino) long remained an isolated token of the artist martyrized by his critics. The portrait of the artist by himself only became a portrait of torture and martyrdom at the end of the nineteenth century. Gauguin then became the convict Jean Valjean and Ensor was led to Calvary. But not many painters were driven to portray this torture.

James Ensor: *The Dangerous Cooks, 1896*

Lampoon

*I've composed this simple, simple,
simple story, to infuriate serious,
serious, serious people.*[1]

Charles Cros

Seen at table in the next room, as if through a window, are from left to right: Edouard Fétis, Eugène Demolder, Camille Lemonnier, Max Sulzberger and Emile Verhaeren, all Belgian writers and critics. Another critic, Theo Hannon, feeling faint, overcome by nausea perhaps, climbs the stairs and makes off. In the kitchen Edmond Picard, holding a frying pan and trident, and Octave Maus with a tray, are busily plying their trade: both are critics. On a shelf above the kitchen range, where the head of the painter Vogels appears to be simmering in the frying pan, are the fish-bodied heads of the painters Lemmen and Van Rysselberghe. Depicted as a plucked chicken, strung up and still laying eggs, is Anna Boch. On a table at the other side of the room is a sucking pig with a monocle, the sculptor Van der Stappen; also a lobster, the painter Henry de Groux. Finally, about to be served up on the tray, cooked and garnished, with eyes demurely shut, is a curious bearded and moustached mermaid lacking a torso. This head has a label stuck in the curly hair, reading: ART ENSOR. The mermaid is a herring, the herring is Ensor. On the kitchen wall a sheet of paper is pinned up. On it is written the title of the picture: The Dangerous Cooks. A lampoon: the portrait of the artist by himself is both derision and challenge.

123

Paul Gauguin: *Self-Portrait with the Portrait of Emile Bernard ("les misérables"), 1888*

Emile Bernard: *Self-Portrait with the Portrait of Gauguin, 1888*

A bonze and "les misérables," correspondence

He looked at himself in the little mirror on his mantelpiece, and said . . .[1]

Victor Hugo

Vincent writes to Theo: "By the way, of course I shall not give anything to Gauguin in exchange for his portrait, because I think that it is sure to be too good, but I shall ask him to hand it over to us for his first month, or as payment for his fare.

"But you can see that if I had not written to them rather strongly, this portrait would not exist, and now Bernard has done one too.

"Say that I was angry, say that it was unjust, but anyway Gauguin has given birth to a picture, and Bernard too."[2]

From Vincent van Gogh to Paul Gauguin: "Your concept of Impressionism in general, of which your portrait is a symbol, is striking . . .

"I have a portrait of myself, all ash-coloured. The ashen-grey colour that is the result of mixing malachite green with an orange hue, on pale malachite ground, all in harmony with the reddish-brown clothes. But as I also exaggerate my personality, I have in the first place aimed at the character of a simple bonze worshipping the Eternal Buddha. It has cost me a lot of trouble, yet I shall have to do it all over again if I want to succeed in expressing what I mean. It will even be necessary for me to recover somewhat more from the stultifying influence of our so-called state of civilization in order to have a better model for a better picture."[3]

From Vincent to Theo: "I have just received the portrait of Gauguin by himself and the portrait of Bernard by Bernard, and in the background of the portrait of Gauguin there is Bernard's on the wall, and vice versa.

"The Gauguin is of course remarkable, but I very much like Bernard's picture. It is just the inner vision of a painter, a few abrupt tones, a few dark lines, but it has the distinction of a real, real Manet.

"The Gauguin is more studied, carried further. That, along with what he says in his letter, gave me absolutely the impression of its representing a prisoner. Not a shadow of gaiety. Absolutely nothing of the flesh, but one can confidently put that down to his determination to make a melancholy effect, the flesh in the shadows has gone a dismal blue.

"So now at last I have a chance to compare my painting with what the comrades are doing. My portrait, which I am sending to Gauguin in exchange, holds its own, I am sure of that. I have written to Gauguin in reply to his letter that if I might be allowed to stress my own personality in a portrait, I had done so in trying to convey in my portrait not only myself but an impressionist in general, had conceived it as the portrait of a bonze, a simple worshipper of the eternal Buddha.

"And when I put Gauguin's conception and my own side by side, mine is as grave, but less despairing. What Gauguin's portrait says to me before all things is that he must not go on like this, he must become again the richer Gauguin of the 'Negresses.'

"I am very glad to have these two portraits, for they faithfully represent the comrades at this stage; they will not remain like that, they will come back to a more serene life."[4]

From Gauguin to Schuffenecker: "I think it's one of my best things: quite incomprehensible (for example), because so abstract. A bandit's head at first glance, a Jean Valjean (Les Misérables) also personifying a despised impressionist painter... The eyes, mouth and nose are like flower designs in a Persian carpet, also personifying the symbolic side. The colours are remote from nature."[5]

From Gauguin to Van Gogh: "The mask of a sturdy, ill-dressed bandit like Jean Valjean, who

Vincent van Gogh: *Self-Portrait as a Bonze, 1888*

has his nobleness and his inner tenderness. The hot blood suffuses the face, and the tones of a fiery forge around the eyes indicate the fiery lava that sets our painter's soul aglow... You have here both my personal image and the portrait of us all, poor victims of society, and it will avenge us by doing good."[6]

Jean Valjean the ex-convict, the outcast, in Hugo's novel *Les Misérables* (1862). Gauguin refers to the passage describing Jean Valjean as he enters the town of Digne, one evening in October 1815:

"A stocky man in the prime of life . . . his hair cropped, yet bristling . . . In his face, a strange composure, humble at first sight, and seeming in the end severe. The eye glowed under the brows like fire under brushwood . . . He was a sinister apparition."[7]

Calling on Monseigneur Bienvenu, Jean Valjean says pointblank: "I'm a convict . . . unwanted by anyone . . . Here's my passport. Yellow, as you see. With these papers I'm driven away wherever I go."[7] Released four days before from prison, where he spent nineteen years as No. 24601 "for having smashed a window pane and taken a loaf of bread."[7]

As an ex-convict Jean Valjean had a yellow passport. Painted yellow is the wall behind Gauguin, on which hangs the portrait of Emile Bernard.

From Vincent to Theo: "Herewith another letter that I wrote about Gauguin's portrait during the last few days. I am sending it to you because I have no time to copy it out, but the chief thing is that I underline this, That I do not like these atrocious hardships of 'the craft,' except in so far as they show us the way. Our way is neither to endure them ourselves nor to make others endure them, but the opposite.

"I do not think I exaggerate about Gauguin's portrait, nor about Gauguin himself."[8]

From Vincent to Theo: "Herewith yesterday's letter which I am sending you, such as it is. From it you will see what I think of Gauguin's portrait. Too dark, too sad.

"I do not say that I do not like it as it is, but he will change, and he must come . . . Once more, one must not do flesh with Prussian blue. Because then it ceases to be flesh; it becomes wood . . . However, I venture to think that with regard to colouring, the other Breton pictures [by Gauguin] will be better than the portrait he has sent me, done, after all, in haste."[9]

Van Gogh is a bonze, Gauguin is Jean Valjean. Both are outcasts, confined to the hermitage or the hulks, to monastery or prison. One withdrawn from the world, the other hounded out of it. Both are poor; no matter whether through choice or compulsion, it is poverty just the same.

The bonze is in Arles, Jean Valjean at Pont-Aven.

Figures! But . . .

"The thing I hope to achieve is to paint a good portrait."[1]

"Tomorrow I am going to Saintes-Maries on the seacoast . . . And to try to get an idea of the figures. For I suppose that all at once I shall make a furious onslaught on the figure, which I seem to be giving a wide berth at the moment, as if I were not interested in it, although it is what I really aim at."[2]

"The figures I do are nearly always detestable in my own eyes, and all the more so in the eyes of others; yet it is the study of the figure that strengthens one's powers most, if one does it in a manner other than the one taught us, for instance, at Mr. Benjamin Constant's."[3]

"The change I am going to try to make in my painting is to do more figures. Altogether it is the only thing in painting that excites me to the depths of my soul, and which makes me feel the infinite more than anything else."[4]

"There is no better or shorter way of improving your work than doing figures."[5]

"I want to do figures, figures and more figures."[6]

"I want to paint men and women with that something of the eternal which the halo used to symbolize, and which we seek to convey by the ac-

Vincent van Gogh:

1. *Self-Portrait with Felt Hat, 1887*
2. *Self-Portrait with Straw Hat, 1887*
3. *Self-Portrait with Hat and Pipe, 1888*
4. *Self-Portrait with Felt Hat, 1887*

Vincent van Gogh:
Self-Portrait with Cut Ear, 1889

But

tual radiance and vibration of our colouring . . . Ah! portraiture, portraiture with the thoughts, the soul of the model in it, that is what I think must come."[7]

"I must say I cannot understand why I don't do studies after the figure, seeing that it is often so difficult for me to imagine the painting of the future theoretically as otherwise than a new succession of powerful, simple portraitists, comprehensible to the general public."[8]

"I always think photographs abominable, and I don't like to have them around, particularly not those of persons I know and love. Those photographic portraits wither much sooner than we ourselves do, whereas the painted portrait is a thing which is felt, done with love or respect for the human being portrayed. What is left of the old Dutchmen except their portraits?"[9]

"I am always finding my best powers frustrated by the lack of models . . . If I went and begged the models – Now do pose for me, I beseech you – I should be behaving like Zola's good painter in *L'Œuvre*.[10]

"I purposely bought a mirror good enough to enable me to work from my image in default of a model, because if I can manage to paint the colouring of my own head, which is not to be done without some difficulty, I shall likewise be able to paint the heads of other good souls, men and women."[11]

"I am working on two portraits of myself at this moment – for want of another model – because it is more than time I did a little figure work."[12]

"They say – and I am very willing to believe it – that it is difficult to know yourself – but it isn't easy to paint yourself either."[12]

Vincent van Gogh:
Self-Portrait, 1889

129

Henri Rousseau:

◁ *The Present and the Past, 1899*

Myself. Portrait-Landscape, 1890 ▷

Clémence and Joséphine

*Shepherdess oh Eiffel Tower the
flock of bridges bleats this
morning.*[1]

Guillaume Apollinaire

It's a quay. Is it a canal? The Ourcq or the Saint-Martin Canal? Is it actually the Seine? Some strollers have stopped on the bank, first a couple, then further away two men with a child. They are contemplating the red reflections in the water of the setting sun, still high, or the flags on the black ship berthed there. Maybe they are gazing at the opposite bank where, behind the opaque foliage of the trees – the pale tree-trunks are visible under the arch of the iron bridge – the façades of buildings can be seen, punctuated with white-curtained windows, grey slate or zinc roofs, and bristling with chimneys.

Almost hidden by all the flags, the Eiffel Tower rises in the pale sky. On the right a grey hot-air balloon ascends among white clouds shaped like folded or crumpled pieces of papier. In the middle stands the painter; round his legs and feet some hesitant repainting is visible. His stiff right arm is pressed against his body; he is wearing a sort of beret edged with red above the greyness of the right temple, similar to the grey of his full beard and moustache. In his right hand, clasped between the outstretched fingers and thumb, is a paint brush. His thumb holds a palette in front of his stomach; his left arm is bent.

The paints, eleven irregular blobs, are aligned next to each other on the edge of the palette which has a couple of words written across it in a cursive hand similar to that of the signature at the bottom left: Henri Rousseau, with the date 1890 beneath it. The signature and the date are written for the picture's spectator; on the palette, the fact that the words are upside down prevents one from reading them off at once. The written words are solely for the painter's eyes; all he needs to do is to turn his hand the other way and reverse the palette so that they are visible to him. The words are names: Clémence and Joséphine. After the conjunction Joséphine is written in a darker patch. (This patch is a passage of overpainting which presumably obliterated another name, no matter what it was.)

These two names, readable by the painter alone, with the blobs of paint acting as a sort of halo for them, are those of his first and second wives. On the 7th of May 1888 Clémence Boitard, whom he had married on the 14th of August 1869, died. On the 2nd of September 1899 he wed Joséphine Noury, herself a widow at the time, who was to die in 1903. These women's names are written out on the palette by which Rousseau proclaims himself a painter. Rousseau was a painter by virtue of these very names crowned by dabs of paint. By "Clémence and Josésphine," in Paris, I am a painter. These names, written for him alone, are both a memento and a dedication. He is a painter both *for* them and *by* them.

The Present and the Past, finished in 1899, is an equivalent proclamation of fidelity. Henri Rousseau and his wife Joséphine are standing in a garden; now, he has only a moustache, but above him in a cloud is his portrait when he was several years younger, then with a beard. Above Joséphine is Clémence's face, her hair parted in the middle.

Clémence and Joséphine depicted together.

130

James Ensor: *Ensor surrounded by Masks, 1899*

Masks

The mask is all.[1]
Delacroix

Masks there are of every kind, with their red mouths groaning or laughing, their eyes no more than empty holes or a stare. On one mask a wig sketches out the hair and another is topped with flowers, a woven crown of leaves, or feathers. These masks are not worn. One, on the left, is atilt, emphasizing the emptiness behind them. These masks are disembodied grimaces and their dense, thronging mob looks as if it is advancing. In the background, or one should say, at the top, the heads between a skull on the left and an inclined cat's head on the right, are smaller. In the midst of this procession, wearing red, a red hat on his head decorated with flowers and a feather, is Ensor as Rubens.

What are these masks? In Ensor's work they are an obsessive presence. They are the masks sold among the seashells in the curio shop of Ensor's grandmother. They are the carnival masks of Ostend, his birthplace, which he never left except to study art at the Brussels Academy from 1877 to 1880. And the mask is one of the *Attributes of the Studio* (1889), as is the palette. They are the *Singular Masks* (1891), which become the *Scandalized Masks* in 1895. In 1901 they reappear as the *Scuffle of Masks*, as before they had figured in the *Entry of Christ into Brussels* (1888), in the *Masks Facing Death* (1888) and in the *Old Woman with Masks* (1889), where again they took the form of a pressing throng of masks.

These obsessive masks surround the painter, press close upon him, harass him. In the print of 1898 which he called *Démons me turlupinant* ("Demons making merry with me"), the engraved demons have the same odious, ridiculous, misshapen faces, and they throng around the painter as the masks do. These demons are no different from those described by thirteenth-century churchmen, such as the Cistercian abbot Richalmus in his *Liber revelationum*, who asserts that we are all surrounded by demons as a man in the sea is bathed by water.[2] St. Anthony tempted is harassed in just this manner.

These oft reiterated masks are the confidants and accomplices of death. The skulls with vacant eyesockets are again masks; and they are the masks of

James Ensor: *Ensor with Flowered Hat, 1883*

death. It was this macabre mask that Ensor wore when he engraved his portrait in 1889, standing with his arm on a mantelshelf, his head no more than a skull. One year earlier Ensor engraved *My Portrait in 1960*: a full-length recumbent skeleton.

And Ensor himself is masked. Ensor seeks to be Rubens. Ensor had already painted himself, in derision, as Rubens: *Ensor with Flowered Hat*. This work is a take-off of the Rubens self-portrait in the Kunsthistorisches Museum in Vienna, but the severe, full and elegant black hat Rubens wears becomes a little flowered hat with two ostrich feathers stuck in it that flop down on the painter's neck.

Ensor is nothing more than this carnival Rubens. Where is the derision? In 1929 Ensor was to be made a Baron by the King of the Belgians, as

Rubens had twice been made a knight, once by the King of Spain and once by the King of England.

The portrait of Ensor surrounded by masks is a variation based on the Windsor Castle self-portrait of Rubens, though Rubens is facing the opposite direction: Rubens turns to the right, Ensor to the left. And the hat worn by Ensor has more of the hats ornamented with flowers and feathers of Suzanne and Helena Fourment than do Rubens' own hats.

Thus Ensor, disguised as Rubens, his hair dressed like that of Rubens' wife or sister-in-law, is masked. A mask in the midst of masks, some of which have eye sockets that are neither hollow nor empty, creating a look for themselves and becoming faces. Ensor's face tends to take on the characteristics of a mask and the masks become faces.

Sir Joshua Reynolds: *Self-Portrait, 1753-1754*

Therese Schwartze:
Self-Portrait, 1888

Questions

Therese Schwartze, who holds in her right hand at an oblique angle an enormous palette and a bundle of brushes, moves her left, with a brush between her fingers, up to her head as an eye-shade; and the shadow of this hand is visible on her face. Her eyes and eyebrows are in the shadow. Like those of Reynolds.

What does this possible link between Therese Schwartze and Sir Joshua Reynolds imply? Is it a tribute? Is it the avowal of an influence? Is it the challenge of seeking to be the equal of the chosen master? Is it the deliberate reference to a justifying example? Does it aim at identification? Is it a mask to be deciphered? What then is the connection between this woman painter and Reynolds?

The answers can only vary.

An anecdote

The painter is standing; his torso is naked under the low-cut V-neck jersey, with the right sleeve rolled up to the elbow and the right fist closed. He holds a palette vertically in his left hand; his black hair is very close-cropped; his clean-shaven cheeks bear only a single shadow of a cheek-bone. The painter looks fixedly and his look strays. What is he looking at?

"Waking up and coming on my reflection in the mirror with my hair all dishevelled, do you know what idea came into my head? You know, I was sorry I wasn't a photographer! It's completely different; that is the way other people see you and the way you see yourself at odd moments in the mirror.

Often in my life I've surprised a facial expression of mine that I've never been able to discover in any of my portraits. And perhaps these were my most genuine expressions. One ought to make a hole in a mirror so that the lens can catch your face at its most intimate, quite unexpectedly."[1]

In November 1918 Pablo Picasso was living in Paris at the Hotel Lutetia. One morning when he was shaving in front of a mirror, somebody told him about Guillaume Apollinaire's death. After that, Picasso was to paint no more self-portraits.[2]

Every morning when he was shaving, it was the sudden news of Guillaume Apollinaire's death, terrible, incomprehensible news, that he saw anew.

Pablo Picasso:
Self-Portrait with Palette, 1906

135

Apostrophe

1915: Every Sunday, P. M. lunches in Blaricum with Salomon Slijper. Blaricum isn't all that far from Laren, in northern Holland, where P. M. works. Salomon B. Slijper orders the artist's self-portrait from Mondrian.

Three years go by. The portrait of the painter by himself has been completed; it's the last portrait. P. M. is to paint no more of them.

The bust is seen in profile: the jacket is of a dark brown; the collar, the stitching, and the folds of the sleeve crossed by stripes of shadow with black accents. The background is a greyish-brown uneven wall. The face, in a three-quarters view, is angled to the left. The pose is similar to one used in a charcoal portrait of 1912. The painter stands in front of one of his canvases hanging on the wall at shoulder height; the frame dents the grey bow-tie he is wearing. The picture displayed is neither signed nor dated, but it may be that date and signature are to be found in the bottom left corner of the picture: it consists of grey, rust-coloured or bistre squares and rectangles behind the painter's head; a darker line frames its contours irregularly. The colours, here more muted, are those of the 1913 *Composition No. 7* in the Solomon R. Guggenheim Museum in New York or of the *Facade in Brown and Grey* in the New York Museum of Modern Art, but the austerity of the composition is entirely different. These rectangles and squares, and the way they are placed, are in the manner of the *Compositions with Pure Colour Planes on a White Ground*. But the picture hanging behind the painter is not one of the canvases of this series – of which the colours would mark the end point. This is no canvas of the series referred to, but the series itself. It was for this series of five canvases that Mondrian created a new signature. These five pictures were signed initially with his early monogram ℍ. But Mondrian painted it out and inserted the new signature, PM, followed by the date 17. Only one canvas in this series, possibly the first, has retained the abandoned monogram. (In 1912 in the catalogue of the exhibition arranged by the Kunstkring in Amsterdam in homage to Gauguin, Mondrian's name appears with that spelling. Up until his death in February 1944 Mondrian was to sign all his canvases PM.)

This portrait of the painter by himself is dated and signed at the bottom left: PIET MONDRIAAN 18.

The signature and the date reject and refuse each other. Both are anachronistic. In 1918 Mondriaan had ceased to exist. The signature dates from before 1912; as early as 1910 Mondrian more often signed P. Mondriaan or ℍ and the first name Piet began to disappear and was seldom seen. And the old signature of 1917 with the monogram taken out, in the compositions with pure colour planes on a white ground, was not to reappear. Thus the year accompanying the signature itself is not the sole element that dates the picture. The form of the signature designates specific periods. Mondriaan country comprises the mills, dunes and beaches of Domburg, the lighthouse towers of Westkapelle, and the church towers of Zoutelande, as well as the farms of Nistelrode, the banks of the Gein and the windmills. This artist named Mondriaan had ceased to exist in 1918.

"Modern man – although a unity of body, soul and spirit – shows us a changed consciousness: all expressions of life are seen in another light; I am thinking of a more positively abstract light.[1] The universal can only . . . find its pure expression when the specific no longer bars the way. Only then can universal consciousness, i.e., intuition, which is the origin of all art, be expressed directly, giving birth to an expression of purified art."[1]

This text which appeared in "De Stijl" is contemporary with the *Compositions* and the self-portrait. Mondrian is governed by the specific. Universal consciousness begins when the painter, "giving birth to an expression of purified art," paints the compositions signed PM.

The signature and the date of this portrait of the painter by himself are not contemporary with each other. Their incompatibility is an apostrophe. The date 18 does not concern the portrait of the painter by himself, but the canvas hanging behind the painter in which his painting begins. The present is eluded and elided. The portrait of the painter by himself is an apostrophe: interpellation and elision. Elision: the signature pushes him back into the past, the date proposes a different kind of painting. Interpellation, the painting displayed which is not a work of the past, a reference quoted; the picture directly above his shoulder is a challenge. This portrait may be read: such was I, my painting is now beginning. But the signature refuses to allow the portrait to be contemporary with it. It must be of significance that this particular portrait is a reply to a collector.

There will be no more portraits of the painter by himself.

Mondrian wanted to hit another target with his pistol: the first portrait he painted of himself in 1900.

Whom is he aiming at? Whom does he wish to kill?

Piet Mondrian: *Self-Portrait, 1918*

Amedeo Modigliani: *Self-Portrait, 1919*

A canvas, a sitting

To be able to work I need a
living person, I need to see him
in front of me.[1]
Modigliani

Modigliani is seated on an ordinary chair in front of a fireplace. Behind him the wall is bare. Nothing on it. A pair of grey-green trousers, a jacket, perhaps of velvet, almost russet-coloured and a foulard knotted round his neck. The shaven face is smooth and unwrinkled. The hair is brown. Modigliani is alone and is posing in front of a mirror. There he sees himself left-handed and paints himself left-handed. His *left* hand, tired, is lying at rest on his thigh; in his *right* hand he holds a paint-stained palette and a few brushes. Presumably he has painted this picture at a single sitting, as he did with all his canvases, and nothing has changed since his return at the outset of this year 1919 from a stay on the Riviera between Nice and Cannes. Jeanne Hebuterne has just returned from there with their daughter. Modigliani is painting himself. His cheeks are hollow, and the pupils of the eyes are not visible. This self-portrait is his first. And Modigliani will shortly be dead.

The empty socket

My painting is autobiographical.
In it I tell the story of my life.[1]
Brauner

"There were quite a number of us there that evening. And there was something that had never happened before: we had gathered together without any real wish to do so or any enthusiasm. That hot August evening was steeped in boredom. Personally I was half asleep and for more than forty-eight hours I had been suffering from a feeling of acute anguish. During my lengthy walk with U the previous day I had experienced an inexplicable and overpowering feeling of fear. My friends began to leave and D, in a state of great excitement, began quarrelling with E. Since it was all in Spanish we understood very little of what was happening. And then, very suddenly, both of them pale and trembling with anger hurled themselves at each other with a violence I do not recall ever having seen. I

Victor Brauner: *Self-Portrait, 1931*

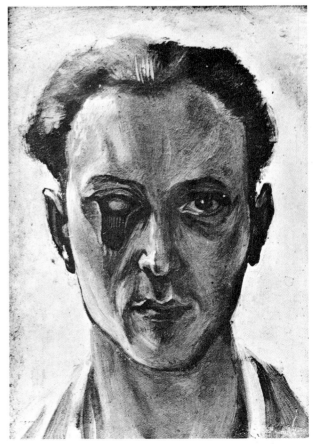

had a sudden presentiment of death and rushed to hold E back. S and U sprang upon D, but the others left, finding things had taken a turn for the worse. D broke loose and I just had the time to catch a glimpse of him when I was felled to the ground by a terrific blow to the head.

"Our friends, who had hastily returned, picked me up to carry me away. Seized by a growing numbness and no longer able to see clearly, I asked to go home and put myself to bed. My friends bore me away, their faces betraying terrible grief and anguish. I was quite unaware of what was happening until during the split second we were passing a wall-mirror, I caught a glimpse of my blood-stained face where the left eye was no more than a huge wound. At that very instant, I suddenly thought about my portrait and in my confused thinking the similarity of the wound heightened my sense of reality and impressed upon me for all time this image that grew in me. I could no longer see. I was lying in the ambulance and my right eye was bathed in blood. And during the operation, both with Dr. G and the friends who had accompanied me, it was only my portrait that I discussed. The doctor confirmed that the eye was gone. That I knew already."[2]

All this happened in Paris on the 28th of August 1938 at 83 Boulevard Montparnasse, in a studio belonging to Oscar Dominguez (referred to by the letter D in Brauner's text of the 7th of November 1944).

Seven years earlier: "One day when I had nothing else to do ... I was not busy with anything, I wanted to do a small picture of myself in front of a mirror, and I painted that portrait.

"To enliven it a little and to make it more extravagant, I removed an eye. Well, it was that very eye which was removed; the actual wound was identical eight years later."[1]

The eye socket is empty. Blood runs over the eye-lid.

In 1944 Brauner wrote in his notebooks: "Now that six and a half years have passed since the loss of my left eye, this mutilation still remains as vivid for me as on the day it happened; it is the most painful and the most important event of my life. As time passes, this event constitutes the paramount turning point of the essence of my vital development."[2]

"This is clearly an event for which one can find no satisfactory explanation."[1]

Death spied out

Francis Bacon: "I've done lots of self-portraits, it's true, because the people around me have died off like flies and there was no one else left to paint except myself. I detest my own face and I've done self-portraits because there has been no one else to paint. But now I've stopped doing self-portraits. I like to paint good-looking people, because I like a good bone structure. I detest my own face but I go on painting it. It's true that ... Every day in the mirror I see death at work, that's one of the nicest things Cocteau said. It's the same for everyone."[1]

No comment.

To paint oneself is to paint the portrait of a man who is going to die.

Francis Bacon: *Self-Portrait, 1973*

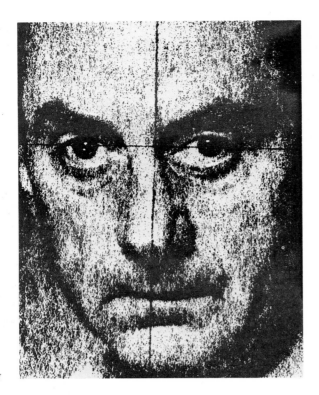

Man Ray:
Self-Portrait, 1971

Aiming: a definition

An ordinary mirror hanging on the wall. A label with black capitals is set in the wall at the height of the white wood frame. Title:

SELF-PORTRAIT

I (whoever looks at the picture is I) looks at Man Ray's self-portrait. I see myself. The mirror is a portrait of Man Ray by himself in which I see myself. Who is Man Ray? Man Ray is myself who am him ... Who is the double?

This mirror hung at a Man Ray exhibition is a self-portrait. But whose self-portrait? The title says nothing of the identity. The self-portrait is a self-portrait. My presence alone gives it an identity. My presence turns *a* self-portrait into *my* self-portrait. My indispensable presence alone gives the work a meaning. This self-portrait, a metaphor of all self-portraits, is it also a metaphor of painting itself, which is dead unless someone looks at it?

The cross of a rifle-sight can be seen against Man Ray's face. The horizontal line traverses the eyes; the vertical line, like a straight scar, marks the forehead, nose and chin.

This face which is looking at me (I haven't changed) is a target; it is the target of all looks.

This self-portrait that the rifle-sight imprints at eye level is a metaphor of all self-portraits on which the eyes are fixed. (Another metaphor: this cross that marks the face is a threat. What assassin is taking aim? The portrait is the portrait of a man who is going to die.)

The portrait of the painter, a portrait by himself, a target, is the point of aim.

The self-portrait is always a mirror in which I aim at myself.

Target and mirror, the definition is given.

Overture

I realized that I am unable not to be myself. I realized that I can never – never, do you understand me? – that I can never stop being myself.
Giovanni Papini
The Fleeing Man

... elsewhere continues the gallery of portraits of painters by themselves. An *anachronistic* gallery: these dated portraits of dead painters refute both time and death and their presence calls forth the memory. Oblivion, as something else, is death again. This gallery is death deceived.

And the prayer intoned there is not
    Requiem aeternam dona eis, Domine
But
    Memoriam aeternam, dona eis, Domine,
    Et lux perpetua luceat eis.
It is they
    Quarum hodie memoriam facimus.
    Fac eas, Domine, de morte transire ad vitam.

And what is repeated by the looks on the faces of the portraits of painters by themselves for those who look at them from century to century, is this other peremptory and assured prayer:
    Recordare quod sum causa tuae viae.[1]

To paint oneself is, in the first place and even beyond any credo, the wish to deny death. And what does it matter if the portrait was painted for an academy, a grand ducal collection, or whether it was done in solitude; or again whether it is a sign of doubt or an assertion of self-confidence? And it is less the answer to the question "Who am I?" or the response to the command "Know Thyself," than a response to that certitude of being someone who will die; and it rejects this certain and hateful death. The central and unending theme is man himself and the portrait of the painter by himself is a metaphor of any work of art, is the will to leave behind an imperishable trace of one's ephemeral self.

Everything else is only a variation of that challenge. It does not matter whether the painter is present at one event or another at the edge of the fresco, altarpiece or canvas; whether he is among his peers or alone as a bust and face devoid of any attributes of painting; whether he is actually painting, and whether what he is painting is visible or not; whether he is with his family; whether he portrays himself as Apelles or St. Luke, a Grand Seigneur or the poorest of the poor. All these variations are a part of history. And the first aim of the self-portrait is to achieve immortality. The history of the self-portrait – and this is a hackneyed paradox – is the motionless history of immortality. The portrait has assumed the outdated forms of a challenge continually taken up and renewed.

Jean-Baptiste Siméon Chardin: *The Monkey-Painter, c. 1740*

The forms of this challenge simultaneously proclaim that they are the rejection of death and a definition of identity. To paint the portrait of someone who is going to die and calls on memory in order not to die, is to paint the portrait of *some unique person who* is going to die. At the same time, it is to paint the essence of identity, to define what the so-called "identity" cards call *distinguishing marks*. The self-portrait is the inventory of those marks. Writing their history is thus simultaneously writing the history of these distinguishing marks, their variations and their gradations. The portrait of the painter by himself and his implicit history of the definition of man and of his links to a particular credo or system, is an implicit history of the specific links, no matter whether they are accepted or rejected.

Le Brun paints himself as the king's first painter; Van Gogh labels himself a bonze. Beyond Le Brun, beyond Van Gogh, what is implicit is the specific place that the Grand Siècle and the Third Republic allotted to the painter; it is this that is highlighted. To write the history of the self-portrait is to write the history of man as a piece in the social puzzle.

And the portrait of the painter by himself is at the same time a metaphor of painting itself and of the specifics by which painting identifies itself. Painting and painter can nowhere else be more interwoven: the painter paints himself as a painter and the painting that he becomes is of his own making. The painter, the model, and the work, bear the same name; and Narcissus looking at himself in the waters of a spring invented painting. Every painter who looks in the mirror at the model he is, is the metaphor of Narcissus all over again, and in this way reinvents painting. The history of the portrait of the painter by himself is the history of painting itself and the reply to this question: who paints what for whom? The history of the artist is the history of the person or entity ordering the work and of the art lover; it is the history of subjects and again it is the history of technique.

In Europe, to write such a history of the immortality and identity of the social body and of painting would require a definition and a verification of each slight difference of meaning. The self-portrait never ceases to be the self-portrait, and this truism implies an additional fact: the self-portrait never ceases to be another self-portrait and the history it writes is a palimpsest.

The foregoing pages, then, can only be the overture to the deciphering of this palimpsest, itself written on the watermarks we have described. Everything remains to be done. The painter is alone, the painter is in the margin of the written parchment, at the edge of the fresco; the painter is surrounded by friends, the painter is a bust and a head, the painter is working, the painter is another. There are scarcely more than a dozen variations of the portrait of the painter by himself, ceaselessly taken up again, from shade of meaning to shade of meaning, from century to century.

And the painter, painter of himself, dependent upon the vectors and waftages of history, has he been nothing more than a trained and performing ape, everlastingly repeating the same thing?

Source references

Numbered references are keyed to the text. Unnumbered references indicate books dealing with the subject of the relevant section.

Lightning conductor (p. 7)

1 PARACELSUS
Liber Paramirum
French translation by Grillot de Givry
Paris 1913.

2 GODARD Jean in
MATHIEU-CASTELLANI Gisèle
Eros baroque
Anthologie thématique de la poésie amoureuse
Paris 1979.

3 CHASTEL André
Lectures at the Collège de France,
Paris 1975-1976.

4 BOCCACCIO, *Livre des Femmes Nobles et Renommées*, MS. fr. 12420,
Bibliothèque Nationale, Paris.

5 *Breviarium cum calendario*,
Österreichische Nationalbibliothek, Vienna.

6 FREUD Sigmund
Ma vie et la psychanalyse, Ch. VI
translation by Marie Bonaparte
Paris 1949.

7 DANTE
Divine Comedy, Inferno, Canto I.

Nuns, monk, man-at-arms
or
The margins of writing (p. 17)

1 VILLARD DE HONNECOURT quoted in
DU COLOMBIER Pierre
Les chantiers des Cathédrales
Paris 1973.

Basso continuo (p. 19)

1 APULEIUS
Apologia
Oxford 1914.

2 ALBERTI quoted by
CHASTEL André
Art et Humanisme à Florence au temps de Laurent le Magnifique
Paris 1959.

3 LEONARDO DA VINCI
Trattato della Pittura
Milan 1939.

4 PAILLOT DE MONTABERT
Traité de la peinture
Paris 1829.

5 ALBERTI Leon Battista
De Pictura, Book II
Milan 1975.

The spring of Narcissus and what flows from it
or
Instructions for use (fiction) (p. 22)

1 ÉLUARD Paul
Capitale de la douleur
Paris 1926.

Epiphany (p. 24)

1 VASARI Giorgio
Delle Vite de' più eccellenti pittori, scultori, ed architettori
Florence 1568.

2 Gospel according to St. Matthew 2.9-11.

3 RÉAU Louis
Iconographie de l'art chrétien
Paris 1955.

4 CHASTEL André
Art et Humanisme à Florence au temps de Laurent le Magnifique
Paris 1959.

5 FRANCASTEL Galienne
Le style de Florence, le Quattrocento
Paris 1958.
CHASTEL André
Botticelli
Paris 1958.
VENTURI Lionello
Botticelli
Vienna 1937.
MESNIL Jacques
Botticelli
Paris 1938.

Pride and Humility
or
Because one is a Painter (p. 26)

1 HEIDRICH Ernst
Albrecht Dürers schriftlicher Nachlass
Berlin 1910.

2 DÜRER Albrecht
Letter to Willibald Pirckheimer,
8 September 1506.
PANOFSKY Erwin
Albrecht Dürer
Princeton 1955.
MÜLLER Wolfgang J.
"Bemerkungen zu Dürers Selbstbildnis von 1484"
Kunstchronik, 1972, No. 10, pp. 344-345.
CHASTEL André
"Dürer, Kunst im Aufbruch"
Proceedings of the Leipzig colloquy
Leipzig 1971.
WINZINGER Franz
"Albrecht Dürers Selbstbildnis"
Zeitschrift für Kunstwissenschaft, VIII,
pp. 63-64, 1954.
La gloire de Dürer
Proceedings of the Nice colloquy, 1972
Paris 1974.
Dürers Gloria. Kunst, Kult, Konsum
Exhibition in the Art Library, Staatliche Museen Preussischer Kulturbesitz, West Berlin, September-November 1971.

All the way to Calvary (p. 28)

1 DÜRER Albrecht
The Painter's Manual (Unterweisung der Messung)
New York 1977.

2 DÜRER Albrecht
Dedication to Willibald Pirckheimer of the Treatise on Proportions.

3 GAUGUIN Paul
Letter to Emile Bernard, August 1889
Lettres de Gauguin à sa femme et à ses amis
Paris 1946.

4 GAUGUIN Paul
Racontars de rapin
Paris 1951.

Painters among philosophers and thinkers (p. 30)

1 VASARI Giorgio
Delle Vite de' più eccellenti pittori, scultori, ed architettori
Florence 1568.
CHASTEL André
Art et Humanisme à Florence au temps de Laurent le Magnifique
Paris 1959.
POIRIER Pierre
La fresque florentine
Paris 1955.

Hypothesis for an etymology and the play on words that comes of it (p. 31)

1 FRAPPIER Jean
"Variations sur le thème du miroir de Bernard Ventadour à Maurice de Scève"
Cahiers de l'Association internationale des études françaises, No. 11
Paris, May 1959, pp. 136-137.

2 PLATO
The Symposium, 208c.

On earth as in heaven (p. 32)

1 Gospel according to St. Matthew 10.38.

2 Gospel according to St. John 12.26.

Abyss (p. 36)

1 CESI Bernardo
Mineralogia sive Naturalis philosophiae thesauri
Lyons 1636.

2 ST. PAUL
II Corinthians 3.18.

3 PLUTARCH quoted in
BALTRUSAITIS Jurgis
Le miroir: essai sur une légende scientifique: révélations, science-fiction et fallacies
Paris 1978.

4 RANK Otto
Die Don Juan-Gestalt
Leipzig 1924
and
Der Doppelgänger
Leipzig 1925.

5 Quoted by STOCKER Arnold
Le Double
Geneva 1946.

Attribute (p.36)

[1] RIPA Cesare
Iconologia
Rome 1593
Quoted from the French edition: *Iconologie ou Explication nouvelle de plusieurs images, emblèmes et autres figures hyéroglyphiques des Vertus, des Vices, des Arts, des Sciences, des Causes naturelles, des Humeurs différentes et des Passions humaines*
Paris 1634.

[2] VAN GOGH Vincent
Letter of 17 September 1888.
TERVARENT Guy de
Attributs et symboles dans l'art profane 1450-1600
Geneva 1959.

Medusa (p. 37)

[1] BELLORI Giovan Pietro
Le Vite de' pittori scultori e architetti moderni
Rome 1672.

[2] OVID
Metamorphoses, Book IV.

[3] MENANDER
The Principal Fragments
Translated by Francis G. Allinson, Loeb Classical Library, Heinemann, London, and Harvard University Press, Cambridge, Mass., 1921. Fragment 538 K.
JOFFROY Berne
Le dossier Caravage
Paris 1959.
FRIEDLÄNDER Walter
Caravaggio Studies
Princeton 1955.
LONGHI Roberto
Il Caravaggio
Milan 1952.
JULLIAN René
Caravage
Paris 1951.

Of Mercury, god, planet and element called Hg
or
The other side of the mirror (p. 38)

[1] MOLIÈRE
Amphitryon, Act I, Scene 2.

Apelles, Lord of Steen (p. 40)

[1] PILES Roger de
La Vie de Rubens
Paris 1681.

[2] Rubens' tomb inscription quoted by
FROMENTIN Eugène
Les Maîtres d'autrefois
Paris 1876.

[3] This tradition is mentioned by Fromentin in *Les Maîtres d'autrefois*: "There side by side, they say, you will find his two wives, and first of all, Helena Fourment – a young girl of sixteen years of age when he married her in 1630, still a very young woman when he died, fair-haired, plump, amiable and sweet-tempered, with very little to cover her charms, naked to the waist." As such, she represents Mary Magdalene in the picture.

[4] Quoted from
STUBBE Achille
Pierre Paul Rubens
Paris 1966.

[5] RUBENS
Letter to Pierre Dupuy, 15 July 1626.
DELEVOY Robert
Rubens
Geneva 1972.
BURCKHARDT Jacob
Recollections of Rubens
London 1950.
FRYNS Marcel
Rubens, Van Dyck, Jordaens
Paris 1962.
PILES Roger de
Dissertation sur les ouvrages des plus fameux peintres
Le Cabinet de Monseigneur le duc de Richelieu. La vie de Rubens
Paris 1681.
OLDENBURG R.
Peter Paul Rubens
Munich and Berlin 1922.
PUYVELDE Leo van
Rubens
Brussels 1964.
STERLING Charles
Rubens et son temps
Paris 1936.
ROOSES Max
L'Œuvre de P.P. Rubens
Antwerp 1886-1892 4 vol.
Catalogue of the Rubens Year exhibition, Antwerp 1977.

In memoriam (p. 44)

[1] VASARI Giorgio
Delle Vite de' più eccellenti pittori, scultori ed architetti
Florence 1568.

Who is laughing? (p. 46)

[1] BACON Francis in
SYLVESTER David
Interviews with Francis Bacon
London 1975.

[2] MATISSE Henri
"Exactitude is not truth", essay in the catalogue of the Matisse exhibition, Philadelphia Museum of Art, 1948, reprinted in Jack D. Flam, *Matisse on Art*, Phaidon, New York and London, 1973.

[3] Gospel according to St. Luke, 15.11-13.

[4] PILES Roger de
Abrégé de la Vie des Peintres avec des réflexions sur leurs ouvrages, et un traité du peintre parfait, de la connaissance des desseins et de l'utilité des estampes
Paris 1699.
BLANKERT Albert
"Rembrandt, Zeuxis and ideal beauty"
Album Amicorum J. G. Van Gelder, 1973.
STECHOW Wolfgang
"Rembrandt Democritus"
The Art Quarterly, VII, 1944, pp. 233-238.
BIALOSTOCKI Jan
"Rembrandt's Terminus"
Wallraf-Richartz-Jahrbuch, XXVIII, 1966, pp. 49-60.
ROSENBERG Jacob
Rembrandt: Life and Work
Cambridge, Mass. 1948.
SCHMIDT-DEGENER F.
Les contradictions de Rembrandt
Antwerp 1945.
WENCELIUS Leon
Calvin et Rembrandt
Paris 1937.

GENAILLE Robert
Rembrandt: Autoportraits
Paris 1963.
ERPEL Fritz
Die Selbstbildnisse Rembrandt
Berlin 1969.
PINDER Wilhelm
Rembrandts Selbstbildnisse
Leipzig 1943.
WRIGHT Christopher
Rembrandt: Self-Portraits
London 1982.
BREDIUS Abraham
revised by GERSON Horst
Rembrandt Paintings
New York and London 1969.

St. Luke (p.48)

[1] VAN GOGH Vincent
Letter B7 to Emile Bernard, June 1888.

[2] DU COLOMBIER Pierre
Les chantiers des Cathédrales
Paris 1973.

The Virgin, the courtesan and the painter
or
Eros frigid (p. 50)

[1] DIDEROT Denis
Salon de 1759, Oxford 1967.

[2] PLATO
The Symposium, 211b.

[3] PLATO
The Symposium, 203a.

La Pittura (p. 51)

[1] RIPA Cesare
Iconologia
Rome 1593
Quoted from the French edition: *Iconologie ou Explication nouvelle de plusieurs images, emblèmes et autres figures hyéroglyphiques des Vertus, des Vices, des Arts, des Sciences, des Causes naturelles, des Humeurs différentes et des Passions humaines*
Paris 1634.
LEVEY Michael
"Notes on the Royal Collection: Artemisia Gentileschi's Self-Portrait at Hampton Court"
Burlington Magazine, 104, 1962, pp. 79-80.

Bourgeois among bourgeois (p. 52)

[1] Quoted in
DESCARGUES Pierre
Hals
Geneva and New York 1968.
SLIVE Seymour
Hals
London 1970.
BAARD H.P.
The Civic Guard Portrait Groups
Amsterdam 1949.
VALENTINER W.R.
Frans Hals
Stuttgart 1923.

Concerning a lock of hair (p. 53)

[1] To Madame Yvonne Deslandres, head of the Centre de Documentation du Costume, Paris, I owe the name by which this stray lock of hair was known in France. G. Dargent also

refs to it as "la cadenette" in his article "A propos du portrait de Simon Vouet au Musée de Beaux-Arts de Lyon," *Bulletin des Musées Lyonnais*, No. 1, 1955, pp. 25-36.

Portrait of Le Nain by Le Nain (p. 54)

1 "Donation réciproque consentie par les trois frères Louis, Anthoine et Matthieu Le Nain de tous leurs biens aux derniers survivants" Archives Nationales Reg. Y, 185, fol. 287 quoted in
Nouvelles archives de l'art français, Vol. IV
Paris 1876.
FÉLIBIEN André
Entretiens sur les vies et sur les ouvrages des plus excellents peintres anciens et modernes
Paris 1688.
GUÉRIN Nicolas
Description de l'Académie Royale des Arts de Peinture et de Sculpture par feu M. Guérin, Secrétaire perpétuel de ladite Académie
Paris 1715.
CHAMPFLEURY
Essai sur la vie et l'œuvre des Lenain, Peintres Laonnois
Laon 1850.
CHAMPFLEURY
Les peintres de la réalité sous Louis XIII, Les frères Le Nain
Paris 1862.
VALABRÈGUE Anthony
Les frères Le Nain
Paris 1904.
GILLET Louis
La peinture au XVIIe et XVIIIe siècle
Paris 1913.
GUIFFREY Jules
Artistes parisiens du XVIe et du XVIIe siècle
Paris 1915.
SAINTE-BEUVE
"Les frères Le Nain, peintres sous Louis XIII"
In *Nouveaux Lundis*, IV
Paris 1865.
JAMOT Paul
Les Le Nain
Paris 1929.
FIERENS Paul
Les Le Nain
Paris 1933.
GILLET Louis
La peinture de Poussin à David
Paris 1935.
STERLING Charles
Peinture française XVIe-XVIIe siècle
Paris 1937.
ISARLO Georges
"Les trois Le Nain et leur suite"
in *La Renaissance*, March 1938, No. 1, p. 158.
ERLANGER Philippe
Les peintres de la réalité
Paris 1946.
LEYMARIE Jean
Le Nain
Paris 1950.
Useful bibliography in the exhibition catalogue *Les frères Le Nain*, Grand Palais, Paris, 1978-1979. See in particular the bibliography of *The Studio*, No. 42, pp. 232-233.

Judith and Holofernes, David and Goliath (questions) (p. 56)

1 The Song of Solomon, 1.3.

Reserve and severity (p. 58)

1 POUSSIN Nicolas
Letter to Chantelou, 7 April 1642 in
Lettres et propos sur l'art
Paris 1964.

2 POUSSIN Nicolas
Letter of 4 February 1646
op. cit.

3 POUSSIN Nicolas
Letter of 28 April 1639
op. cit.
BLUNT Anthony
"Poussin Studies: Self-Portraits"
Burlington Magazine, August 1947.
DORIVAL Bernard
"Les autoportraits de Poussin"
Bulletin de la Société Poussin, June 1947, p. 39.
TOLNAY Charles de
"Le portrait de Poussin par lui-même au Louvre"
Gazette des Beaux-Arts, XCIV, 1952, tome 2.
CHASTEL André
Actes du colloque international Nicolas Poussin CNRS 1958
Paris 1960, 2 vols.
BLUNT Anthony, THUILLIER Jacques
Nicolas Poussin et son temps
Exhibition, Musée des Beaux-Arts
Rouen 1961.
SCHNEIDER Pierre
Le voir et le savoir. Essai sur Nicolas Poussin
Paris 1964.
GIDE André
Poussin
Paris 1945.
BLUNT Anthony
The Paintings of Nicolas Poussin: A Critical Catalogue
London 1966.
THUILLIER Jacques
Nicolas Poussin
Novara 1969.

The key and the cross (p. 60)

1 VALLENTIN Antonina
Goya
Paris 1951.

2 Proceedings of the colloquy *Velázquez, son temps, son influence*
Casa de Velázquez 1960
Paris 1963.
LASSAIGNE Jacques
Velazquez: les Ménines
Paris 1973.
CLARK Kenneth
Looking at Pictures
London 1960.
STIRLING-MAXWELL W.
Velázquez and his Works
London 1855.

Morituri... (p. 66)

1 SHAKESPEARE
Hamlet, Act V, Scene 1.

**The abbot and the grand duke
or
The request and the order** (p. 70)

1 *Au siècle de Louis, l'heureux sort te fit naistre./Il luy fallait un peintre, il le fallait un maistre.*
Lines by Quinault engraved on Edelinck's print after Largillière's portrait of Le Brun.

2 LE BRUN Charles
quoted in JOUIN Henry
Charles Lebrun et les arts sous Louis XIV. Le premier peintre, sa vie, son œuvre, ses écrits, ses contemporains, son influence
Paris 1889.

3 PILES Roger de
Abrégé de la Vie des Peintres...
Paris 1699.

4 Letters quoted in
JOUIN Henry, op. cit.

5 LACOMBE-BAUDRAND Henri de
Mémoire de Mr Baudrand sur la vie de Mr Olier et sur le séminaire de Saint Sulpice
Paris 1682.

Posthumous assassination (p. 72)

1 MOLIÈRE
La Gloire du Val de Grâce
Paris 1669.

2 PILES Roger de
Abrégé de la Vie des Peintres...
Paris 1699.

3 LE BRUN Charles
quoted in MARCEL Pierre
La Peinture française au début du XVIIIe siècle, 1690-1721
Paris c. 1906.

4 THUILLIER Jacques
Introduction to the exhibition catalogue
Les Peintres de Louis XIV
Lille 1968.

5-6 *Archives de l'art français (première période)*
Paris 1851-1862.

7 DUSSIEUX, SOULIÉ, DE CHEN-NEVIÈRES, MANTZ, DE MONTAI-GLON
Mémoires inédits sur la vie et les ouvrages des Membres de l'Académie royale de peinture et de sculpture publiés d'après les manuscrits conservés à l'Ecole impériale des Beaux-Arts
Paris 1854.

8 GUÉRIN Nicolas
Description de l'Académie de peinture et de sulpture, 1715-1781, par son secrétaire Nicolas Guérin et par Antoine Nicolas Dezallier d'Argenville le fils
Paris 1893.

9 Exhibition catalogue, *Pittura francese nelle collezioni pubbliche fiorentine*, Palazzo Pitti
Florence 1977.

10 PERRAULT Charles
Les hommes illustres qui ont paru en France pendant ce siècle
Paris 1696.

11 D'HAUDICQUER DE BLANCOURT
Nobiliaire de Picardie
Paris 1693, p. 412.

12 The three noble parts: "Invention, drawing, colouring" (note by Molière to his *La Gloire du Val de Grâce*, Paris 1669).

13 PETERSON Karen and WILSON J. J.
Women Artists
New York 1976.

14 CHÉRON Elisabeth Sophie
La Coupe du Val de Grâce
Paris 1700.
THUILLIER Jacques
Introduction to the exhibition catalogue
Les Peintres de Louis XIV
Lille 1968.

CHAMSON André
Preface to the exhibition catalogue *Chefs-d'œuvre des Musées de Province*
Paris 1958.

**Medals and a hunting picture
or
Portrait of an office** (p. 76)

1 GUÉRIN Nicolas
Description de l'Académie de peinture et de sculpture, 1715-1781, par son secrétaire Nicolas Guérin et par Antoine Nicolas Dezallier d'Argenville le fils
Paris 1893.

2 DUSSIEUX, SOULIÉ, DE CHEN-NEVIÈRES, MANTZ, DE MONTAI-GLON
Mémoires inédits sur la vie et les ouvrages des Membres de l'Académie royale de peinture et de sculpture...
Vol. II: *La vie de M. Desportes peintre d'animaux, écrite par son fils, conseiller de l'Académie royale de peinture et de sculpture, lue en l'Assemblée le 3 août 1748*
Paris 1854.

3 COYPEL Charles Antoine, quoted in
MARCEL Pierre
La Peinture française au début du XVIIIe siècle, 1690-1721
Paris c. 1906.

Studio (p. 78)

1 LESTHÈVE Jacques
La vie quotidienne des artistes français au XIXe siècle
Paris 1968.

2 LEROY Alfred
La vie intime des artistes français au XVIIIe siècle de Watteau à David
Paris 1949.

**Comedy
or
From one mirror to another** (p. 80)

1 FIELDING Henry
Joseph Andrews, Preface
London 1742.

2 HOGARTH, quoted in
MAYOUX Jean-Jacques
English Painting from Hogarth to the Pre-Raphaelites
Geneva-London-New York 1972.

3 SHAKESPEARE
As You Like It, Act II, Scene 7.

4 SHAKESPEARE
Hamlet, Act III, Scene 2.

5 HOGARTH, quoted in
MAYOUX Jean-Jacques
op. cit.

6 SHAKESPEARE
Macbeth, Act V, Scene 5.

The eye deceived (p. 82)

1 FÉLIBIEN André
L'idée du peintre parfait, pour servir de Règle aux jugements que l'on doit porter sur les Ouvrages des peintres
London 1707.

2 HEIDRICH Ernst
Albrecht Dürers schriftlicher Nachlass
Berlin 1910.

3 VASARI Giorgio
Delle Vite de' più eccellenti pittori, scultori ed architetti
Florence 1568.

4 DIDEROT Denis
Salon de 1759
Oxford 1967.

5 DIDEROT Denis
Salon de 1763
Oxford 1967.

6 VASARI Giorgio
op. cit.

7 PILES Roger de
Abrégé de la vie des peintres...
Paris 1699.

8 FRANCASTEL Galienne and Pierre
Le Portrait. 50 siècles d'Humanisme en peinture
Paris 1969.

9 LESTHÈVE Jacques
La vie quotidienne des artistes français au XIXe siècle
Paris 1968

10 BRAQUE quoted in
CHARBONNIER Georges
Le monologue du peintre
Paris 1959

Portrait of the gaze: eye to eye (p. 84)

1 DIDEROT Denis
Salon de 1781
Oxford 1967.

From the motif (p. 84)

1 ECKERMANN J.P.
Gespräche mit Gœthe, 21 December 1831.
IRWIN David
"Jacob More, Neo-classical Landscape Painter"
Burlington Magazine, 1972, p. 775.

**Goya at the Spanish court
or
The rise of a new dynasty** (p. 86)

1 GOYA, letters quoted in
VALLENTIN Antonina
Goya
Paris 1951.

2 GOYA, letter quoted in
MANCERON Claude
Le bon plaisir: les derniers temps de l'aristocratie, 1782/1785,
Vol. 3 of *Les hommes de la liberté*
Paris 1976.
MALRAUX André
Saturne
Paris 1950.

Allusive headgear (p. 89)

1 VIGÉE-LEBRUN Elisabeth, quoted in
HAUTECŒUR Louis
Madame Vigée-Lebrun, peintre de Marie-Antoinette
Paris 1908.

Faithful (p. 93)

1 VIGÉE-LEBRUN Elisabeth, quoted in
VIALLET Bice
Gli Autoritratti femminili delle R.R. Gallerie degli Uffizi in Firenze
Rome c. 1920-1930.

2 VIGÉE-LEBRUN Elisabeth
Souvenirs, Vol. 1, p. 110
Paris 1835-1837.

3 *Correspondance des Directeurs de l'Académie*,
Vol. XV, p. 372
Paris 1906.

4 Exhibition catalogue,
De David à Delacroix, la peinture française de 1774 à 1830
Paris 1974.
HAUTECŒUR Louis
Madame Vigée-Lebrun
Paris 1914.
PETERSEN Karen and WILSON J. J.
Women Artists
New York 1976.

Tumour (p. 95)

1 DAVID Jacques-Louis
Discours du citoyen David, député du département de Paris sur la nécessité de supprimer les académies, 8 août 1793
Paris 1793.

2 Quoted in
DAVID Jules
Le peintre Louis David
Paris 1880.
HOLMA K.
David, son évolution et son style
Paris 1940.
ROSENAU Helen
The Painter Louis David
London 1948.
VERBRAEKEN René
Jacques Louis David jugé par ses contemporains et par la postérité
Paris 1973.

Drawing and nature (p. 96)

1 INGRES quoted in
COURTHION Pierre
Ingres raconté par lui-même et par ses amis
Geneva 1947.

2 INGRES quoted in
TERNOIS Daniel
Preface to *Tout l'œuvre peint de Ingres*
Paris 1971.

**Second digression
in which Poussin's self-portrait as copied
and modified acts as a manifesto** (p. 100)

1 INGRES quoted in
COURTHION Pierre
Ingres raconté par lui-même et par ses amis
Geneva 1947.

2 INGRES quoted in
DELABORDE Henri
Ingres, sa vie, ses travaux, sa doctrine d'après les notes manuscrites et les lettres du Maître
Paris 1870.

3 POUSSIN Nicolas
Lettres et propos sur l'art
Paris 1964.

4 Proceedings of the Dürer colloquy at Nice, 1974, *La Gloire de Dürer*, article by
STREIDER P.
"La signification du portrait chez Dürer."

Solitude and hard times (p. 104)

1 FLAUBERT Gustave
Dictionnaire des idées reçues
Paris 1913.

2 HUGO Victor
Les Misérables, III, Book V, 1
Paris 1862.

3 LESTHÈVE Jacques
La vie quotidienne des artistes français au XIXe siècle
Paris 1968.

The story behind the portrait (p. 106)

1 COURBET Gustave
Letter of May 1854 quoted in
BOREL Pierre
Le roman de Gustave Courbet, d'après une correspondance originale du grand peintre
Paris 1922.

2 RIMBAUD Arthur
"Perfumes do not make his nostrils quiver;/He sleeps in the sun, his hand on his chest/Quietly. He has two red holes in his right side."
"Le dormeur du val," *Poésies*, XVIII
Paris 1946, Pléiade p. 66.

3 NERVAL Gérard de
"In St. Pélagie prison/Under this reign enlarged,/Where musing and pensive/I live a captive,/No grass grows/and not a sprig of moss/Along the walls barred/and newly cut."
"Politique 1832," *Poésies*
Paris 1960, Pléiade.

4 "Puisque réalisme il y a," quoted from
COURBET Gustave
Letter to Champfleury, autumn 1854
Printed in the exhibition catalogue *Gustave Courbet*,
Grand Palais, Paris 1977, p. 246.

St. Gudula and St. Sophia (p. 115)

1 Letter quoted in the exhibition catalogue
Pittura francese nelle collezioni pubbliche fiorentine,
Palazzo Pitti
Florence 1977.
ROSENBERG Pierre
Philippe de Champaigne
Paris 1968.
THUILLIER Jacques and CHATELET Albert
French Painting from Le Nain to Fragonard
Geneva and New York 1964.

Orders and decorations (p. 116)

1 INGRES quoted in
COURTHION Pierre
Ingres raconté par lui-même et par ses amis
Geneva 1947.

2 LECOMTE Jules
Le perron de Tortoni, indiscrétions biographiques
Paris 1863.

3 INGRES quoted in
DELABORDE Henri
Ingres, sa vie, ses travaux, sa doctrine...
Paris 1870.

4 ANGRAND Pierre
Monsieur Ingres et son époque
Paris 1968.

5 HUGO Victor
"Good taste is an iron gate./Beware of long-standing good taste!/At all times its curry-comb/Has set Pan, the sacred goat, a-bleating!
" Taste dockets, isolates, picks out,/And for fear of revels,/Puts locks and bars/Around everything here below.
"It cloisters, and says I set free./It cuts off, and says I have created./Be sober is its principle,/Well suited to the sick.
"It's the cousin of envy,/It's a member of the senates./To the heart and life, it gives/The form of a padlock."
Toute la Lyre
Paris 1859.

6 Reminiscence of AMAURY-DUVAL in
COURTHION Pierre
Ingres raconté par lui-même et par ses amis
Geneva 1947.
PICON Gaëtan
Ingres
Geneva-New York-London 1980, new edition.
MERAS Mathieu
Colloque Ingres
Montauban 1967.
WILDENSTEIN Georges
Ingres
London 1954.
AMAURY-DUVAL Eugène
L'atelier d'Ingres
Paris 1878.

Which model? (p. 119)

1 DELACROIX Eugène
Journal, 31 March 1824
Paris 1935-1938, 3 vols.

2 DELACROIX Eugène
Journal, 9 June 1823.

3 DELACROIX Eugène
Journal, 14 May 1824.

4 CÉZANNE quoted by Alberto GIACOMETTI in
CHARBONNIER Georges
Le monologue du peintre
Paris 1959.

5 GIACOMETTI in CHARBONNIER.
MOREAU-NÉLATON Etienne
Delacroix raconté par lui-même
Paris 1916, 2 vols.
FLORISSOONE Michel
Eugène Delacroix
Paris 1938.
STARZYNSKI J.
"En quête des autoportraits de Delacroix entre 1849 et 1853"
Gazette des Beaux-Arts, 1964, p. 245.
DESLANDRES Yvonne
Delacroix
Paris 1963.
ROBAUT Alfred
L'œuvre complet de Delacroix
Paris 1885.

Martyrdom (p. 122)

1 MICHELANGELO quoted in
MARNAT Marcel
Michel-Ange, une vie
Paris 1974.

Lampoon (p. 123)

1 CROS Charles
"Le hareng-saur," *Le Coffret de Santal*
Paris 1970, Pléiade p. 138.

A bonze and "Les Misérables": correspondence (p. 124)

1 HUGO Victor
Les Misérables, Book VII, 3
Paris 1862.

2 VAN GOGH Vincent
The Complete Letters, 3 vols.
Thames and Hudson, London, and New York Graphic Society, 1958
Letter 544 to Theo, Arles, September 1888.

3 VAN GOGH, letter 544a to Gauguin, Arles, September 1888.

4 VAN GOGH, letter 545 to Theo, Arles, September 1888.

5 GAUGUIN Paul, letter to Emile Schuffenecker, October 1888, quoted in
CACHIN Françoise
Gauguin
Paris 1968.

6 GAUGUIN, letter to Van Gogh quoted in
CACHIN.

7 HUGO Victor
Les Misérables, Book II, 1-6
Paris 1862.

8 VAN GOGH, letter 546 to Theo, Arles, October 1888.

9 VAN GOGH, letter 547 to Theo, Arles, October 1888.

Figures! But... (p. 126)

1 VAN GOGH Vincent
The Complete Letters, 3 vols.
Thames and Hudson, London, and New York, Graphic Society, 1958
Letter Wl to his sister Wilhelmina, Paris, summer-autumn 1887.

2 Letter 498a to A.H. Koning, Arles, June 1888.

3 Letter B8 to Emile Bernard, Arles, late June 1888.

4 Letter 516 to Theo, Arles, August 1888.

5 Letter 517 to Theo, Arles, August 1888.

6 Letter B15 to Emile Bernard, Arles, early August 1888.

7 Letter 531 to Theo, Arles, August 1888.

8 Letter B19a to Emile Bernard, Arles, late October 1888.

9 Letter W14 to his sister Wilhelmina
St. Rémy, late September/early October 1889.

10 Letter 543 to Theo, Arles, September 1888.

11 Letter 537 to Theo, Arles, 17 September 1888.

12 Letter 604 to Theo, St. Rémy, September 1889.

Clémence and Joséphine (p. 130)

1 APOLLINAIRE Guillaume
"Bergère ô tour Eiffel le troupeau des ponts bêle ce matin."
Alcools
Paris 1965, Pléiade.

Masks (p. 132)

1 DELACROIX Eugène
Journal, 16 May 1823
Paris 1935-1938, 3 vols.

2 ABBOT RICHALMUS quoted in
COMBE Jacques
Jérôme Bosch
Paris 1946.
FIERENS Paul
James Ensor
Paris 1943.
HAESAERTS P.
James Ensor
Brussels 1957.
TANNENBAUM L.
James Ensor
New York 1951.

An anecdote (p. 135)

1 BRASSAI
Conversations avec Picasso
Paris 1964.

2 BRASSAI, p. 147.
PICASSO
"Déclarations"
Cahiers d'Art, X, No. 10, 1935.
Exhibition catalogue *Hommage à Picasso*
Paris 1966, Grand Palais, Petit Palais, and
Bibliothèque Nationale.

ZERVOS Christian
*Catalogue général des œuvres de Pablo Picasso
1895-1963*
23 volumes
Paris 1952-1971.

Apostrophe (p. 136)

1 *La Nouvelle Plastique dans la peinture dans " De
Stijl" I, 1917-1918*
Translated by Michel Seuphor
Paris 1956.
SEUPHOR Michel
Piet Mondrian, sa vie, son œuvre
Paris 1956, new edition 1970.
Exhibition catalogue *Mondrian*
Orangerie des Tuileries, Paris 1961.
JAFFÉ H.L.C.
Piet Mondrian
New York 1970.

A canvas, a sitting (p. 138)

1 Quoted in
MODIGLIANI Jeanne
Modigliani sans légende
Paris 1961.

The empty socket (p. 138)

1 BRAUNER Victor
Talks with Max-Pol Fouchet
TV broadcast, Terre des Arts, Paris 1960.

2 BRAUNER Victor
Notebooks quoted in the exhibition cat-
alogue *Victor Brauner*
Musée d'Art Moderne, Paris 1972.
MABILLE Pierre
"L'œil du peintre" in
Minotaure, No. 12-13, Paris 1939.
JOUFFROY Alain
Brauner
Paris 1959.

Death spied out (p. 139)

1 BACON Francis
*L'art de l'impossible
Entretiens avec David Sylvester*
Geneva 1976.

Overture (p. 140)

1 Grant them, Lord, eternal rest
Grant them, Lord, eternal memory,
And may light perpetual shine upon them
Those whose memory we today recall,
Make them, O Lord, to pass from life to death
Remember, for me hast thou come.
These lines are from the Requiem Mass.

Acknowledgments

Much help has been received at every stage of this work, most of all from Franck Popper, a faithful guide and adviser.

I owe thanks to Madame Claude Ducourtial, curator of the Musée National de la Légion d'Honneur in Paris, and Madame Dupaquier for identifying the orders and decorations worn by this or that figure; to Mademoiselle Yvonne Deslandres, director of the Centre de Documentation du Costume, for information about the style of dress worn by the painters portrayed here; and to Dottoressa S. Meloni, head of research at the Uffizi Gallery in Florence, for further information.

Without the friendly cooperation of Monsieur and Madame Roger Boulez, librarians at the Ecole Supérieure in Paris, of Mesdemoiselles C. Maurice and D. Barrau and Monsieur A. Macaire, and without the help of Madame S. Tricoire who deciphered my manuscript, and that of Madame Ledannois, I could not have carried the work through to its conclusion: I am most grateful to them all.

For translations of Russian and German catalogues, my thanks are due to Madame Tatiana Grenier and Monsieur Otto Schauer.

Several members of the medical profession have kindly elucidated certain details indispensable to a full understanding of some of the portraits reproduced here.

List of Illustrations

Index of Names

SKIRA

Book design and layout by
Lauro Venturi

Text and plates printed by
IRL Imprimeries Réunies Lausanne S.A.

Binding by
Mayer & Soutter S.A., Renens/Lausanne

Printed in Switzerland